THE
EVERYTHING.
ELOPEMENT
BOOK

Avoid the wedding chaos!

Shelly Hagen

For the brides out there who are
dreaming about escaping the wedding.

An Everything® Series Book.
Everything® and everything.com are registered trademarks of
F+W Publications, Inc.

Published by Adams Media, an F+W Publications Company
57 Littlefield Street, Avon, MA 02322 U.S.A.
www.adamsmedia.com

ISBN: 1-58062-027-X

Printed in Canada.

J I H G F E D C B A

Library of Congress Cataloging-in-Publication Data
Hagen, Shelly.
The everything elopement book / Shelly Hagen.
p.   cm.   (Everything series book)
ISBN 1-59337-027-X
1. Weddings–Planning. 2. Elopement. I. Title. II. Series:
Everything series
HQ745.H18   2004
395.2'2–dc22   2003019602

This publication is designed to provide accurate and authoritative information with regard to the subject matter covered. It is sold with the understanding that the publisher is not engaged in rendering legal, accounting,
or other professional advice. If legal advice or other expert assistance is
required, the services of a competent professional person should be sought.
—From a *Declaration of Principles* jointly adopted by a
Committee of the American Bar Association and
a Committee of Publishers and Associations

Many of the designations used by manufacturers and sellers to distinguish
their products are claimed as trademarks. Where those designations appear
in this book and Adams Media was aware of a trademark claim, the designations have been printed with initial capital letters.

Illustrations by Dave Winter.

This book is available at quantity discounts for bulk purchases.
For information, call 1-800-872-5627.

Welcome to the
EVERYTHING® series!

THESE HANDY, accessible books give you all you need to tackle a difficult project, gain a new hobby, comprehend a fascinating topic, prepare for an exam, or even brush up on something you learned back in school but have since forgotten.

You can read an *EVERYTHING*® book from cover to cover or just pick out the information you want from our four useful boxes: e-facts, e-ssentials, e-alerts, and e-questions. We literally give you everything you need to know on the subject, but throw in a lot of fun stuff along the way, too.

We now have well over 150 *EVERYTHING*® books in print, spanning such wide-ranging topics as weddings, pregnancy, wine, learning guitar, one-pot cooking, managing people, and so much more. When you're done reading them all, you can finally say you know *EVERYTHING*®!

Ⓔ **FACTS:** Important sound bytes of information

Ⓔ **ESSENTIALS:** Quick and handy tips

Ⓔ **ALERTS!:** Urgent warnings

Ⓔ **QUESTIONS:** Solutions to common problems

THE
EVERYTHING
Series

Dear Reader,

Are wedding bells driving you mad? Would you rather drive nails into your forehead than discuss the guest list with your mother? Are you having trouble coughing up a grand for a wedding cake?

You're not alone. These days, many brides are realizing that a wedding is what you make of it—it doesn't have to follow the Typical Wedding Formula in order to be special. Your vows can take place somewhere other than a church. You're not obligated to have 200 vaguely familiar relatives in attendance. You don't have to wear a hand-beaded wedding dress with a fifteen-foot train.

Eloping is a viable choice for couples who want to avoid the hassle and cost of the typical wedding. You've seen the movies with the woman escaping from her bedroom window into the arms of her Prince Charming. That's not what this book is about. It's about planning a truly alternative wedding—one that you can look back on without regretting having paid for 300 dinners, twenty of which went uneaten.

Shelly Hagen

THE

EVERYTHING
Series

EDITORIAL

Publishing Director: Gary M. Krebs
Managing Editor: Kate McBride
Copy Chief: Laura MacLaughlin
Acquisitions Editor: Bethany Brown
Development Editor: Julie Gutin
Production Editor: Jamie Wielgus

PRODUCTION

Production Director: Susan Beale
Production Manager: Michelle Roy Kelly
Series Designer: Daria Perreault
Cover Design: Paul Beatrice and Frank Rivera
Layout and Graphics: Colleen Cunningham,
Rachael Eiben, Michelle Roy Kelly,
Daria Perreault, Erin Ring

Visit the entire Everything® series at everything.com

Contents

Acknowledgments

Writing an elopement book seemed like a hefty task, until I asked for (and received) a little help along the way. Thanks to my agent, Jessica Faust, and to my editors at Adams, Bethany Brown and Julie Gutin—each of you gave me invaluable input and feedback. Special thanks to Karyn Shanks Ulrich and to Karen Hill, who went out of their way to help me pull some pieces together. Thank you to the brides and grooms who gave me the lowdown on their own weddings and elopements so that others could live up to their examples, or learn from their mistakes. And finally, thanks to Mike, the man I eloped with, for dealing with the frenzy that can only mean a deadline is drawing near.

The Top Ten
Elopement Checklist Items

1. **Tickets.** Please don't rush to the airport for your quickie elopement trip without your airline tickets.

2. **Wedding outfit.** Will you say your vows in a fancy dress, a classy suit, or shorts and a tank top?

3. **Marriage license.** You can't say, "I do" without one, so pack it in a secure but easily accessible spot.

4. **PDA or address book.** You may need it for calling friends and family from the road.

5. **Contact information.** In the event that someone needs to find you, consider leaving your hotel number with a *trustworthy* friend.

6. **Camera.** You want some precious keepsake photos? Do it yourself—or snag a friend or witness to snap some pictures of you and your new husband.

7. **Rings.** So small—and so easy to forget.

8. **Vows.** It took you weeks to find the right words, so make sure you have them written down.

9. **Fortitude.** You'll need it when you start thinking about telling your families about your elopement.

10. **The groom.** You can't get married without him!

Introduction

WEDDINGS CAN SET OFF a flurry of strong feelings in the bride-to-be. If she's not lost in her daydreams of being Princess for a Day, chances are she's sweating out the enormous amount of details involved in planning the event. Anyone who's ever been involved in a wedding—from the lowliest bridesmaid to the mother of the bride—knows that traditional weddings are expensive, time consuming, and wrought with emotional battlefields.

Dealing with the necessary contacts (the photographer, the caterer, the dress shop) can leave the bride with swirling numbers in her head while she's trying to function in her everyday life. She may take to wandering around her workplace muttering strange equations to herself. "How can a dress with four yards of fabric cost four thousand dollars? No, that can't be right. One yard of fabric costs a *lot* less than a thousand dollars."

Putting together a guest list that pleases everyone can be another potential minefield for the betrothed couple—especially if they're the ones footing the bill and would rather not invite their parents' coworkers. Otherwise sane mothers of the bride or of the groom may lose their faculties and start demanding lobster wrap appetizers and the more expensive champagne for the reception—which, by the way, has grown to 450 guests so that your stepmother's entire family could also be invited. She's the oldest of thirteen siblings, so her younger sisters and brothers also want to bring their toddlers. You understand.

If you're about to lose your will to go on with this production, it's time to get back to the basics. What is it that you want your wedding to be? Some brides love the hoopla and general craziness that surrounds even the best-planned wedding. But other brides can't stand being the center of attention and may see a large wedding as a huge waste of time and money. If this second type of bride sounds more like you, eloping may be just the remedy you need to cure that wedding planning–induced heartburn.

Planning your elopement may sound like a contradiction in terms. Upon hearing the word *elopement*, many people envision a couple secretly running away in the middle of the night, much to the chagrin of both families. Fortunately for you, times have changed, and eloping is now considered less of a jailbreak and more of an incredibly romantic—and financially sound—way to tie the knot. There are many ways to make your elopement serve the dual purpose of being easy on your mind (and wallet) and also being the special, individualized wedding that you want.

Take some time to really give thought to what you feel is important for your wedding. There are so many options available to the modern bride, make sure that the wedding you choose suits *you* first—you can worry about what your family will think after you make that determination.

Chapter 1

No Stress, No Hassles

Planning that Big Wedding can take up your entire life, and the wedding itself might take on a life of its own. Some brides despise the hassles of a large wedding and being the center of attention. They don't feel like they should be subject to old traditions and don't feel the need to be the center of attention even for a day. If this sounds even remotely like you, think twice before committing yourself. You may be better off eloping.

Your Real Wedding Persona

There are so many aspects of wedding planning that can drive you crazy—and for the most part, they're details that will hit you from out of nowhere. You can plan way in advance, but there are some things you can't safeguard against. There's little you can do about a last-minute cancellation by the limo driver, for example. Some women thrive under pressure; some women prefer to avoid it. If you despise aggravation in your everyday life, don't expect your attitude to change simply because you're planning your wedding.

Ⓔ QUESTION?

Do you hate getting lots of attention in your everyday life?
If you are the type of person who hates getting a surprise office birthday party, it may be *incredibly* irritating to you to have strangers hovering over you while you just want to smooch your honey. Eloping may be a better option for you.

Quiz: Large Wedding versus Elopement

Are you really prepared to plan a large wedding, or would you be better off planning to elope? Before you make your decision, take the following quiz and *be honest* with yourself. It just may help you make the decision that's right for you.

1. At your reception, it seems that every male guest wants to dance with you. Your response?

   a.   "Gee, my feet really hurt."
   b.   "Gladly, kind sirs."
   c.   "Get away from me right now."

If you plan the Big Wedding, you'll be expected to spend the evening catering to your guests' whims—even though it's supposed to be *your* day. If you answered *a* or *c*, you may not enjoy being a traditional bride.

2. The week before your wedding you turn on the news to see that your cake maker has been arrested for tax evasion. You:

   a.   Cry. And then you keep on crying some more.
   b.   Call the police and tell them to throw the book at her for ruining your wedding.
   c.   Opt to bake your own cake—or maybe brownies.

Women who choose *c* as their answer are hereby given the green light to plan any size wedding they choose—these are the women who aren't going to be bothered by anything. Most brides would react by shedding countless tears. Ask yourself if you can handle any major last-minute glitches.

3. Your mother's golf league has been invited to the wedding and they've given you a joint gift—golf clubs for you and your husband, along with a membership to the most exclusive golf course in the area. You don't golf. Your reaction:

a. This is a perfect excuse to *learn* how to golf.
b. This is a hugely expensive gift that you feel uncomfortable accepting.
c. You cannot believe these women would spend this type of money on you—they don't even know you.

If you plan a large wedding, be prepared for lots of gifts. If you think you might feel funny accepting overly generous gifts from your parents' friends—and then writing the accompanying thank-you notes—you may want to avoid the scene and elope.

4. Everyone is staring at you. You *are*, of course, walking down a long aisle on the arm of your dad, and you *are* wearing a white dress. You feel:

a. Like a princess.
b. Like a fool.
c. Incredibly uncomfortable. (You wish one of the groomsmen would do something foolish to avert all those eyes away from you.)

If you're leaning toward *b* or *c*, you don't like being the center of attention. Eloping makes it a party of two—

you will only be the center of your new husband's attention, and you're probably all right with that.

5. You're choosing your wedding meal from the caterer's menu, when the following thought strikes you:

 a. "I really like shrimp."
 b. "I really like chicken."
 c. "Am I actually going to be able to sit down and eat at my reception?"

The last answer is rooted firmly in reality. Many brides get so caught up in the vortex of the reception—the pictures, the greetings, the conferring with the Mother of the Bride—that they aren't able to eat dinner at all. If you think you'd rather concentrate on your new husband over a quiet wedding dinner, eloping may be a great option for you.

6. At family gatherings, your sister loves pulling out the camera. First, she makes you pose with Uncle George. Then, she arranges the entire family in a pyramid. Next, it's you alone—in profile. Every time it happens, you want to:

 a. Pout and preen for the camera.
 b. Fix your hair and powder your nose for posterity.
 c. Permanently affix that camera strap to her neck.

What's this? You chose *c*? You're not alone. Some women hate having their pictures taken, and even those who enjoy the occasional family photo find that being forced to say "cheese" for hours on end is highly annoying. When you elope, you probably won't hire a professional photographer—and even if you do, you won't spend your entire wedding day faking a smile while you pose with guests who are actually strangers to you.

7. At your high school reunion, you came face to face with old acquaintances and their new husbands and wives. When it was time for small talk, you:

a. Found things to talk about and had a lovely time.
b. Stood there in awkward silence grasping at conversational straws.
c. Excused yourself early and went home.

Some women truly love to get to know new people and find that any opening in a conversation is worth pursuing. Other women hate small talk so much, they would much rather spend an evening alone than even attempt to make chitchat with strangers. If you answered *b* or *c*, you belong to the latter category. Consider this: When you elope, the only thing you'll *have* to say is "I do."

8. You've got the engagement ring. How long are you willing to wait for the wedding band to make things official?

a. As long as it takes to book that ballroom in the big hotel.

b. As long as it takes to book that caterer you want.

c. As long as it takes to find someone who'll pronounce you husband and wife.

If you answered *c*, you're definitely ready to elope. To you, the wedding is about taking that man you're in love with to be yours forever—it's not about the food or even the location. If waiting a year (or more) just so you can have a fancy meal with hundreds of guests seems like a ridiculous idea, you're already on the eloping track.

9. At your wedding, you see every single member of your extended family, including all of your obnoxious cousins and your surly Aunt Judith. Your reaction?

a. "It's so nice to have the whole family together."

b. "I hope Aunt Judith has a good time—she sure needs it."

c. "I hope I can avoid Aunt Judith—she never has a single nice thing to say about anybody."

What are you thinking, honestly? If you're leaning toward *c*, don't beat yourself up for having mean thoughts. You want to share this day with your new husband, not the most grating members of your extended family. You're thinking of an intimate wedding, which sounds like an elopement by any stretch of the imagination.

10. You're dressing for your Big Wedding and the room is full of bridesmaids, none of whom seem to be interested in helping you. In fact, they seem to be more concerned with their own reflections in the mirror than with your impending vows. Your likely reaction:

a. You ask nicely for help with your dress.
b. You throw a hissy fit because they're being negligent in their duties.
c. You ask yourself, "Why did I ask these women to be bridesmaids? I knew this would happen."

If you have a pretty good feeling that your bridesmaid candidates may lead you to a major wedding meltdown, ditch the maids and the rest of the wedding party. Who needs them? Just grab your guy and go—you're definitely ready to elope.

Ⓔ ALERT!

Being completely honest with yourself is the key to evaluating your tolerance for common Big Wedding hassles. If you think you just aren't up for this kind of circus and you're thinking how nice (and how romantic) it would be to get married without countless worries, nuisances, and stress factors, a simple elopement might be your dream wedding.

Fewer Details to Contend With

The most obvious reason to choose eloping over the Big Wedding is the hassles inherent in planning it. You come home from work expecting peace and quiet, and what do you find instead? An answering machine blinking madly. The dressmaker called. Can't find those buttons you wanted for the bridesmaid dresses, plus she's going out of town for a month, so she'll get back to you—sometime. The caterer called. Since you've chosen salmon for the reception and there's a salmon shortage this year, it's going to cost roughly triple what the original quote stated. Oh, and the rabbi called, too. Seems as though he has this fundraiser to go to and he won't be able to make it to your wedding. He thinks maybe the Baptist church has an opening that day; maybe you could convert.

In Others You Trust

When you're planning a Big Wedding, there are a lot of people you need to rely on, and last-minute crises can leave you out in the cold on your wedding day—literally.

A few years ago, a bridal dress shop in a northeastern city burned down to the ground. The fire took place on a weekday, when the shop had dresses for weddings scheduled for that weekend. The affected brides were understandably upset; the dress shop owner was quoted in the newspaper as calling these women "crybabies."

Is that story enough to make your hair stand on end? When you involve any outside party in a big event like a wedding, there's a chance of things going wrong. It's a gamble that almost always pays off for the most part—really horrible things like the dress shop fire seldom happen. However, many brides have their own horror stories that involve caterers skipping town, banquet halls being closed down by the Health Department, or blizzards that shut the entire state down on their wedding weekend. If you want to avoid the hassles and the potential letdowns, why not consider eloping?

Ⓔ ESSENTIAL

When you choose to elope, there may still be a mishap or two, but on a much smaller scale. Your life savings will presumably not be speeding down the road with your nefarious caterer, and you will spend far less time and energy correcting a misspelled name on your wedding license than you will trying to book a new banquet hall on a week's notice.

Come As You Are

Depending on the type of elopement you choose, you can dress as casually as you like. Marty eloped to Maine with her fiancé and dressed very low-key for the ten-minute ceremony. "Our witnesses dressed up in their Sunday best," she laughs, "and there we were, in shorts and sandals. But hey—it was July and hotter than heck, and I wanted to be comfortable. Plus, I would have felt silly in a lacey dress on this particular beach. It was more like a picnic area."

That was twelve years ago and proof positive that a bride does not need a $1,500 dress to live happily ever after.

Wedding Burritos for Two

How did Marty and her new husband celebrate their marriage? Just as casually. "We took a long walk on the beach afterward and didn't even think about dinner until we were hungry. Then we decided on the restaurant that looked best to us. Very last-minute, completely spontaneous, and possibly the best dinner I ever had."

They didn't have to feed an army of relatives, and they actually got to look at each other over their wedding dinner—instead of leaving their meals to pose for pictures.

On Your Timetable

While many couples opt to plan a Saturday wedding in the year 2012 (the first date available at the atrium in the grand hotel downtown), you just can't see that happening. What is the point of dragging this engagement out, you're wondering, when you just want to marry him?

Weddings are literally being run by the availability of wedding services—so instead of getting married in the fall, as you've always hoped to do, you're being forced into a winter wedding, because there's simply not a reception site in town with an open date until January.

Or you can wait until the following fall—at which point you will have been engaged nearly eighteen months.

Eloping, on the other hand, can be as easy as hopping a plane to Vegas, where a couple can say, "I do" immediately after receiving their marriage license. Even if you decide to elope in a state where there is a waiting period, it's still not going to take you a year (or two) to plan your nuptials. You can get married and get on with your life together instead of having to deal with the purgatory of being engaged for what may start to seem like forever.

Ⓔ FACT

Twenty-six states have a mandatory waiting period between filing for a marriage license and saying, "I do." The states with the longest period are Minnesota (five days) and Wisconsin (six days). Washington, D.C., also has a five-day waiting period.

A Peaceful Wedding Vibe

No waiting also means that there will be less time to go head-to-head with your mom (or his mom) in the event that she's not particularly happy with your choice of mate or with the type of wedding you want. If you've found the man you want to marry, to heck with the dissenters. You're old enough to make your own decisions.

Yes, your mom will be mad when you come back from your elopement, but she was going to give you a hard time anyway. You've spared yourself at least several months of prewedding hell and forced her into accepting your marriage—or not. It's done, and that's that. You've gotten the ball rolling toward the situation's final resolution, and you didn't have to suffer through her threats of boycotting your wedding.

When the Future Is Uncertain

You may also have more practical considerations. What if you just don't know where you'll be a year from now? How can you plan a Big Wedding if, for instance, your fiancé is in the military and may be shipped off to another location in a few months? If you've put several thousand dollars into your wedding and you or your baby are shipped overseas to an undisclosed location in the meantime, you can kiss that money goodbye.

Ⓔ ESSENTIAL

If your long-term schedule is uncertain and you don't want to risk your hard-earned cash on a wedding that might not happen, eloping is a great option. You can always plan a ceremony—a *renewal* of your vows—for a time when you're absolutely certain that you'll both be able to attend.

The Spotlight Is Off

Hosting a Big Wedding will put you at center stage. You need to decide if you want that starring role, keeping in mind that it's a role for which you need to rehearse and wear a smile so tight your face will start to ache. You won't have an understudy on the Big Day—there will be no escape. So, are you really ready to be the star of your wedding show?

Being the center of attention is exactly what some couples want, though many of these couples live in Hollywood and court the attention from the media. You and your honey may not feel this way, especially where your wedding is concerned. If you only have eyes for each other and hate to be interrupted when you're having a quiet evening alone, it's understandable that you'd want to keep your wedding as low-key as possible.

Stop Looking at Me!

Some brides genuinely hate being on display. But from the moment you put that wedding dress on, people will start to stare; they'll smile at you continuously and expect you to be beautiful and happy every single second of the entire day. The poor bride literally cannot use the restroom without everyone inquiring after her and pointing out to one another: "There she is! She's going to use the toilet!"

This is part of the territory with the Big Wedding and the reception that follows. These concerned individuals are your guests. They have come to see you and your groom tie the knot, wish you well, and watch you dance with your dad. You will be outnumbered. You will not have one second to yourself. You may not see your groom for the duration of the reception, as his long-lost uncle may take this opportunity to fill your new hubby in on his hitchhiking adventures over the last twenty years.

Everyone wants to be near the bride and/or groom, as though you possess some good luck that might transfer onto your guests. Folks also expect that every bride wants this attention. (After all, you wouldn't have invited all of these people if you didn't—*right?*)

Ⓔ FACT

Most elopements have a minimal amount of photography—just enough to capture the essence of your special day. Consider this: If you have a big family, you'll spend the better part of the evening smiling at the camera.

Smile—Again!

It's likely that your wedding day will be captured on film. There'll be people with video cameras and more people taking pictures. In fact, they'll try to capture your every move for posterity. If you're a model—or feel like one—you're going to love this. If, on the other hand, you're not comfortable having your own personal paparazzi for the day, all that picture taking will get real old, real fast.

Picture this scenario: A bride who doesn't really want to have a Big Wedding, dressed up in a gaudy getup of her mother's choosing, having her picture taken every two minutes by an incredibly expensive photographer that she and the groom really can't afford. Sounds like something you're interested in?

Guilt Gifts

If the idea of being in the spotlight is making you think twice about having the Big Wedding, what about the fact that you'll be showered with gifts by people you hardly know? As nice as it may be to receive wedding gifts, it also feels odd to some brides to receive lavish gifts that they feel they hardly deserve.

Kara was married last year, and she had a big, traditional reception. "I couldn't believe how generous some of our guests were, and I couldn't believe how *badly* I felt about it. I didn't invite these people—my parents did—and even though I know my parents do the same thing at their friends' kids' weddings, it didn't feel right to me. I could tell they were bored, they were putting in their time until they could leave, and they felt obligated to spend a set amount of money on a gift."

Of course, there's absolutely nothing wrong with accepting a gift from a guest you barely know. They don't have to give you anything; that's their decision. But if you just don't feel right about it, that's another issue altogether. When you throw in the possibility that your parents' friends most likely feel obligated to attend your wedding because your parents came to *their* daughter's wedding, it kind of kills the sentiment of any gift you've been given.

Eloping takes care of the guest list and lets those friends of your parents off the hook. They are not going to feel as obligated to send you a gift if they haven't had to schlep all the way to your reception. Likewise, you won't have to feel badly about them being there when you know they'd rather be somewhere else.

Ⓔ QUESTION?

Will you really have the patience to meet and greet with all the guests at your wedding?
Remember, when you invite several hundred guests to a reception, you are expected to touch base with each and every one of them. If you're not up to that, if you really want to spend your wedding day with your guy, think elopement.

Not for Wallflowers

A big part of the Big Wedding reception is the dance party that ensues after dinner. People will expect to see you and your groom boogie up a storm. You may think that you will be excused from this activity because, as a rule, you don't cut a rug, but your guests may not care. They will not give credence to your excuses. They will want to see you out there doing the bus stop and the chicken dance and generally acting goofy.

If the idea of the First Dance makes you panic, you're definitely ready to elope. That way, you won't have to suffer through the electric slide, the Macarena, or the polkas—unless you and your new hubby hit the clubs on your own.

Breaking Traditions

Dancing is just one of the many traditions you may prefer to skip altogether. But there are many traditions out there that your parents may just insist on having at your Big Wedding. Let's talk about our Polish brides. Some of them may have to suffer through the dollar dance, during which gentlemen guests pin a dollar on the bride's dress for the pleasure of dancing with her.

Then there's the always lively and lovely smashing of the cake into one another's faces. *And* you've got the hokey pokey, the throwing of the bouquet, the removal of the garter, and the limbo to contend with.

All of these things are actually great fun for the bride and groom who are playful and enjoy being the center of attention in any setting. However, the bride and groom who feel that following wedding traditions diminishes the individuality of a wedding are going to regret allowing some of the more obnoxious traditions to take place at their wedding. If you're finding yourself wondering just how you're going to escape from partic-ipating in these traditions, a better solution may be eschewing *all* tradition and eloping instead.

Wedding Chitchat Avoided

Etiquette states that as the bride, you are required to let a line of guests come to you to wish you well, and you are expected to circulate at your reception to make sure all the guests are enjoying themselves. It *does not matter* that you don't know most of your guests—your dad's entire office and the guys he plays basketball with, your mom's golf league and the neighbors you lived next door to when you were in kindergarten. Everyone who has ever heard your name is there, as well as a bunch of people who would have no idea who you were if you weren't wearing that particular dress.

If making small talk with complete strangers for the better part of your wedding reception turns you on, you're all set. Get your jaw loosened up, because it will be flapping nonstop for hours. But if you're not into chitchatting, think about how nice it would be to say your vows and only have your new husband to turn your attention to.

Religious Issues

What if your parents expect you to be married in the church that you attended as a child—except you don't go to church anymore, and you have absolutely no intention of having a religious ceremony? Or perhaps you've converted to another religion and it's a huge point of contention in your family, even more so now that your wedding is looming on the horizon. Or maybe you and your fiancé come from different religious backgrounds.

One great way to take care of your marriage lickety-split is to elope. Look at it this way: Your parents are going to be upset if you have a Big Wedding without the benefit of their religion. *You* are going to be upset if you cave in to their demands.

It's your wedding. By eloping and choosing your own officiant, you're taking control of your vows. Sure, your parents might still be upset when you arrive home married, but you will have made your own choices—and the question of who is going to marry you and your husband will be a dead issue.

Is There Anything More Romantic?

While your wedding will be the defining moment in your relationship, the actual planning and execution of the day can be anything but romantic. In fact, you may feel like you've completely lost sight of what your wedding is really about, while simultaneously losing sight of your groom.

Ⓔ ALERT!

If your wedding planning is making you and your groom miserable, there's something amiss. If you're planning a Big Wedding, make sure that it's really right for both of you. You wouldn't want your wedding to be the thing that breaks up your relationship.

Less Time for Arguments

After several months of arguing over how much you're going to spend, where the reception should be, and who should and shouldn't be invited, you may start to feel like an old married couple—and not necessarily a *happily* married one. Getting married is supposed to be the best and most romantic time of your life together. The wedding is supposed to bring you closer to each other. It's not supposed to be the impetus for arguments that leave the two of you not speaking to each other for weeks on end.

Eloping erases the stress of so many wedding factors—the finances; the bombardment of choices from the caterer, the tuxedo shop, the cake lady; your future mother-in-law's insistence on inviting the groom's former girlfriend, whom she considers "an old friend of the family." When you forget about the nitty-gritty details, you let romance rule your wedding day.

Anyone Seen My Groom?

How do you want to remember your wedding day? If you can already sense that a Big Wedding is going to go by in a flash and you'll barely remember anything about it, maybe you want to go with Plan B and elope.

It's so much more romantic to be able to be together *all day* on your wedding day, instead of being constantly separated by a barrage of well-meaning guests and that pesky photographer who wants to take far too many pictures—"Men over here! Ladies, wait over there!"

If it's extremely important to you that you and your groom have a lot of time to be together on your wedding day, eloping is a surefire way, and maybe the best way, to guarantee it will happen.

Consider Your Priorities

Many couples want to get married and they just don't care how it happens. They're willing to let their mothers dictate the terms and traditions so long as someone is going to pronounce them man and wife by the end of the day.

 FACT

> Eloping can take any form. It's *your* creation. You can get married where you want with or without guests and at the hour of your choosing and celebrate in any manner afterward. Everything in your elopement depends on your own ideas and how creative you want to be. And creativity, of course, is the root of romance.

If you want to have an absolutely original wedding day from start to finish, eloping is a great option. No matter how hard a couple tries, most traditional weddings follow the same basic pattern, which is fine for the couple who wants that, of course. But when you choose to elope, you throw the pattern out the window.

Chapter 2
Not Everything's Relative

Mothers, fathers, siblings, friends—they bring such joy into your life. So why are they driving you insane as you try to plan your wedding? Your mom has suddenly become opinionated and wants to be a part of your every single wedding-related decision. Your dad has a new girlfriend he plans on bringing to the reception. And your bridesmaids are rallying against your every move. Are they all trying to convince you that eloping is your best option? That may just be it.

Mamma Mia!

Is your mom turning into some sort of wedding-planning monster? You're not alone. Many brides find that their sweet mothers start losing their minds once they hear the words "reception" and "mother of the bride." It seems that some mothers take the liberty of planning the wedding *they* would have had if they had been able to control their own mother way back when. How can you nip this in the bud? Cruel as it may sound, you might need to rip your wedding out of her hands.

Mom's Gone Mad with the Checkbook

Are your parents ready to pay for every wedding expense, provided they have final approval on your choices? Natalie had this experience with her mom. She says: "My mom and I had always had a good relationship, and she and my dad were paying for the wedding, so I thought nothing of asking for her opinion on certain things. It became very clear early on in the planning that she was going to choose everything—the country club, the time of day, my dress, my bridesmaids. She honestly couldn't see why she *shouldn't* have the last word on everything, since she was paying for it.

"I couldn't take it. I didn't want my wedding to be an ordeal that hurt my relationship with her, so I eloped. I realized that this wedding was going to cause big trouble between us, and I had seen what my friends went through with their moms and the hard feelings that it all caused. Plus, I didn't care about matching tablecloths or having my cousins as bridesmaids. I had a simple civil ceremony, which was just fine with me."

Ⓔ ESSENTIAL

> If the wedding is a "gift" from your parents with obvious strings attached, you may want to reconsider going down this particular aisle. It's going to be your mother's dream wedding, not yours. If that's going to cause more trouble than it's worth, think about how nice it would be to get married without those strings.

Natalie had a choice to make. Should she allow her mother to plan a wedding Natalie didn't want, since her parents were financing it, or should she pop her mom's bubble and just get hitched? For Natalie, though, the choice was obvious. She is very happy she chose eloping, and eventually her mother accepted her choice.

Mom Is Your New Adversary

It's shocking how the most mild-mannered mothers can suddenly reveal a monstrous, nasty side in the midst of wedding planning. They argue with the bride, insisting that *no one* gets married at three in the afternoon. They criticize the groom's choice of attendants. They threaten not to attend the June ceremony if the bridesmaids are going to wear burgundy dresses, because that's clearly a fall color.

These mothers have an entirely different angle on the whole wedding. They're *not* paying for it, and yet, they have an opinion on everything. No one is quite sure why these ill-behaved mothers feel it's their right to run amok. The reason doesn't matter. If your mother (or your guy's mother) is turning your wedding planning into an absolute trial, eloping is a great way to pull the reins in on her.

Ⓔ FACT

In the end, eloping may not repair the relationship, especially if the mom in question has really gone off the deep end. But you will look back and know that you did what you felt was right for you, which may be the most important thing when you're getting married.

Step Problems

You've got your mom, your dad, your stepmom, your stepdad, your siblings, and your half siblings involved in different areas of the wedding, and various relatives serving as your bridal attendants—and you haven't even started thinking about the groom's family at this point. The nontraditional family is the norm for many clans. Everyone is expected to adjust, and those who can't get along are kept at a distance from one another. Until your wedding day, that is.

Are Those War Cries You Hear?

If Mom and Dad went through a bitter divorce, no one expects them to have a lot of nice things to say about each other. Everyone understands that they don't want to eat Sunday dinner together. However, when it comes to your wedding, you would hope (and should expect) that both of them will keep a civil tongue in their head and just do what they're asked to do.

It shouldn't take a U.N. resolution to declare peace between these people for the duration of your reception. If the backbiting started the minute you announced your engagement (your mother has opined—loudly—that your father should not be allowed to walk you down the aisle, lousy bum that he is; your father has told you that he just can't be in the same room with "that woman" and hopes you understand that he won't be coming to the reception), ask yourself why you're doing all of this.

The answer, most likely, will be that you want to be married with your friends and family looking on and giving you their support. If they're not giving you anything but grief, you may be better off hitting the road with your fiancé and getting hitched somewhere quieter.

Dueling Moms

It happens sometimes that a stepmother will overstep her boundaries and try to usurp the mother of the bride role. Of course, your mom isn't going to stand for that, and your dad isn't going to stand for your mom not standing for that.

Anything you say to anyone under these circumstances will be misunderstood and misconstrued, because no matter how good your relationship with your stepmother has been up until now, your mom is going to expect your loyalty, and your stepmother is going to be crushed when you do what your mom demands of you.

These are wounds that take a long, long time to heal. When you think about it, none of this was your doing to begin with, but you will bear the burden of choosing sides if it comes down to that. Is packing a bag with a little veil sounding pretty good right about now? Thought so.

Ⓔ ALERT!

Remember the cardinal rule of weddings: Emotions run high and previously sane people go nuts. You're already walking a fine line here, trusting that your parents will behave for one day—even though they've never been able to do it in the past. Save yourself. Err on the side of caution. Grab your man and go.

Two Families to Deal With

Maybe you didn't realize that when you accepted your fiancé's proposal (or he accepted yours), you agreed to join his family. It may sound trite and old-fashioned to you, but that's the reality of your situation. If you're just now discovering how nutty his family is—and that they really *aren't* nuts about you—you may be wondering how you're going to pull off a classy wedding without one of his relatives, like his dad, dropping his trousers at the reception just to make you cry.

Don't feel as though you have to stand your ground and force his family to attend a wedding they aren't completely thrilled about just to prove your point. You're going to be dealing with these people for a long, long time. If you think they're going to sabotage your wedding day (intentionally or just by being themselves), don't give them the opportunity. Eloping gives you the chance to marry your man in peace, without constantly keeping an eye on what his family members are up to at the reception. Of course, this admonition applies to your own family as well.

The Whole Family's Here

It's bad enough dealing with all the parents, but wait until you get the rest of your crazy families together. It's time to admit the truth—there are family members out there that just plain get on your nerves. Your Aunt Tess may mean well, and she doesn't have a mean bone in her body, but she just makes you feel as though you're still an awkward twelve-year-old. Do you want to feel icky at your wedding when she starts asking about your acne medication?

Here Comes the Wedding Police

It's bad enough your mom has to invite every last relative, but she had to invite the most opinionated (and, quite frankly, *miserable*) aunts and uncles of the bunch. Brides around the world find themselves highly irritated by wedding guests who find something to complain about at the reception. The drinks are watered down. That dress isn't very flattering on you. Did you have to seat them near the kitchen? Where's the cake, anyway? You call *that* a cake?

ESSENTIAL

> Some brides can handle criticism just fine; others take it very personally. If you fall into the second category and you have a family full of unsolicited advice givers, *run*. You will regret approving their names on the guest list, and it's a sure method for establishing long-term hard feelings.

Who Invited *You*?

Like it or not, some people (mothers, in particular) feel that weddings are the perfect place to mend old family feuds. So you haven't spoken to your cousin Betty since she borrowed $1,000 from you and used it to start an escort service? Great news! She's just been paroled and your mother thought it would be terrific for the two of you to get together this Saturday and talk this whole thing out. Never mind the fact that you've got a slew of other activities planned for your wedding day—this is family! Of course, no one can choose, or control, their family members. You couldn't have kept Betty out of jail.

However, it is your decision whether or not you want to mend that bridge or burn it.

Unfortunately, family elders often have different plans. The only way to prevent an interfering matriarch from attempting to bring the family back together over a nice wedding meal is to either slap a piece of industrial-strength tape over her mouth or to keep the wedding on the q.t.

Where's the Bride?

Here's another scenario that may sound familiar. You're the quiet one of the family, the sibling who fades into the background while your brothers and sisters relish the spotlight during holiday dinners. No one notices when you go outside to sneak a smoke (tsk, tsk), and when it's time to leave, you're accustomed to hearing the phrase, "Oh, Honey, you were so quiet, we forgot you were here!" Family gatherings are not that much fun for you.

Unfortunately, your wedding is looking like it could turn out to be just another boring family reunion. Those throngs of relatives honestly wouldn't notice if you vanished from the face of the earth, and yet, they'll all come to your wedding. Unfortunately, once again they're there to see your parents and siblings. You, meanwhile, will unhappily revert back to your role in the family as the Invisible Woman (although you will be quite visible in your wedding garb).

Ask yourself if you might be happier—and feel a whole lot more grown up—getting married outside the scope of this particular family situation. Make it *your* day instead of a day for the rest of your family to get together and chitchat without noticing that you're sitting in the corner wearing a big white dress.

This Is Your Sister's Wedding Year

Your sister—or your cousin, or your future sister-in-law—has already announced her engagement and was quite peeved to hear that you plan to wed this year, too. You're crowding her out of the spotlight, a spotlight that you really don't have much interest in. After all, you're getting married because you want to be with your guy forever. She seems to be far more determined to put herself on display for her entire engagement period.

No one is suggesting that you should allow a sibling or friend like this to force you into choosing another wedding date or into having a completely different type of wedding than you want. Unless she has, in fact, been named Supreme Ruler of the Universe, you can and should do what you want.

However, wouldn't eloping be a great way to get her off your back and legitimately draw some of that spotlight back toward you? You'll come home married and she, meanwhile, will still be acting like Bridezilla. One of you will be a happy bride; the other will reap what she sows.

Attendants from Hell

The traditional wedding most often includes a lovely procession of bridesmaids. There goes the first one, the second one . . . was that bridesmaid number ten you just saw walking down the aisle? Well, it couldn't be helped, as the bride has a virtual army of sisters. Then again, she had to leave the groom's sister out, and she's in trouble now!

Ⓔ ALERT!

Choosing bridesmaids can be a nightmare, but the bridesmaids themselves can also reveal a stunning aptitude for making you wish you'd never met them—even if they're family.

Picking and Choosing

Everyone has seen a wedding party that was just a little too large. Twelve bridesmaids? Definitely excessive. But have you ever taken the time to wonder how that bride ended up with such a huge line of attendants? Did her mother guilt her into including every cousin on both sides of the family? Does her fiancé have eight sisters—and all of them helped raise him? Does the bride herself come from a very large family?

The thing with having so many bridesmaids is that you will never be able to make them all happy, and bridesmaids have a way of making the bride miserable. And it gets even worse when the bridesmaids are relatives, because you really can't exclude anyone from the wedding lineup without starting a family feud that will last for decades.

The Process of Elimination

So what happens when you choose not to include one (or some) of your relatives or a family member from the groom's side in the bridal party? You will be cast as Demon Bride, the power-hungry cruel Woman in White, dictating who gets to wear taffeta and who doesn't.

It sounds ridiculous, and yet it's true. When you start eliminating family from your pool of potential bridesmaid candidates, it will affect your relationship with them for years to come. When Connie was planning her wedding to Gerald, for example, she decided not to ask Gerald's sister to be in the wedding. She explains: "His sister was *always* out-and-out mean to me. She was so rude to me. She wouldn't even speak to me when we had dinner at their mom's house. And when we told his family we were engaged, she just stood there with this look on her face, like 'Oh, great.'

"She never congratulated us, she never asked about the wedding, and I really didn't feel it was my responsibility to ask her to be in my wedding. I felt like if I asked her, after she had always treated me so badly, that she would always treat me that way, because it would have been like bending over backwards to accommodate this girl who obviously didn't like me. And since she obviously didn't like me, I didn't think *not* asking her would be a big deal.

"I also knew that she would complain about everything—the dress would be too expensive, the color would be wrong, she wouldn't want to buy the shoes. I didn't want to deal with that."

This sounds like a clear-cut case of self-preservation on Connie's part. His sister had treated her badly from day one, and would continue to treat her badly no matter what, so why would she go looking for trouble by including her sister-in-law in the wedding party?

Ⓔ FACT

A bridesmaid's primary responsibilities are hosting the bridal shower and attending to the bride on the day of the wedding. If you've been living on your own for years and really don't need plates and a blender, you may see a shower as kind of ridiculous, anyway, so why not skip it?

Unfortunately, neither Connie's sister-in-law nor her future mother-in-law saw it that way. Gerald's mother had a huge fit when she learned that her daughter would not be traipsing down the aisle in a bridesmaid dress—and the sister-in-law started to treat Connie even worse than she had in the past. "I thought Gerald's family dinners were uncomfortable before," she says. "You could have cut the tension with a knife when all of this happened."

What did this do for family relations? Nothing good. Connie says, "Gerald and I paid for our wedding, so I didn't think his mother had any right to butt in, even if it was on her daughter's behalf. I was pretty annoyed by her attitude about the whole thing. Plus, it wasn't any secret that Gerald's sister hated me—the whole family knew it. But I was the bad guy for not including her. Let's just say that it took *years* to mend this rift. And even now, when the subject of our wedding comes up and his mom or sister are around, there's always an awkward silence."

If Connie could go back and include the sister-in-law, would she? "No," she says. "But having gone through all of that, if I were getting married now, I would honest-to-God think about eloping, just to avoid the family stuff."

Bridesmaid Warriors

Although bridesmaids are supposed to be the proverbial gust beneath the bride's wings, almost every bride can come up with a horror story or two about the members of her wedding party. Bridesmaids can get the wind up their skirts and pull all kinds of stunts you never thought possible—from the familiar "I refuse to wear that dress," to the more creative "I really hate your fiancé, but I guess I'll be in the wedding anyway because I look good in pink," to the absolutely bizarre "I won't be coming to the reception because I just hit it off with the limo driver. If you need me, I'll be out in the car with him."

Ditch the Maids

If you can see where this whole thing with your friends is going to go as soon as they start wearing their

Bridesmaid banners, you may be better off with just one attendant at your elopement—or without any. Take Andrea's situation, for example. She has four sisters, her husband has three, and Andrea also has two cousins who pretty much grew up in her house. "I thought having nine bridesmaids would be no big deal—*because* they were all family—and up till that point, they had all been very well behaved."

Ⓔ ESSENTIAL

If you need a witness in the particular state you're eloping in, you can choose anyone to be your witness during your elopement—your best friend, an acquaintance, a coworker. Because elopements are often last-minute affairs, you'll have to go with the flow and pick the person who is available and willing to go along with it.

The trouble started when Kimberly, one of Andrea's future sisters-in-law, announced that she wouldn't be able to make it to the bridal photo sessions immediately preceding the wedding. Her boyfriend's college graduation was that morning and she wanted to attend. "I started thinking, *She's never going to make it back in time for the wedding,*" Andrea recalls, "so there wasn't much point to her being in it. So I nicely told her that if she was going to the graduation, she shouldn't try to fit serving as a bridesmaid into her day, too. Which started World War Three."

In addition to Kimberly's jam-packed agenda, Andrea soon learned that her own sisters felt the proposed bridesmaid dresses were "tacky" and were angling to wear frocks of their own creation. They even went so far as to purchase fabric for a "mock-up" of the dress they planned on wearing.

How did Andrea solve this mess? You guessed it. She left, on a jet plane. She came home married, dismissed the bridesmaids, and lived happily ever after.

Best of the Best

When you elope, you don't have to have endless conversations about which color looks best on all of the girls you've chosen as bridesmaids. You also don't have to worry about what type of dress will flatter the tall, the short, the skinny, and the not-so-skinny attendants.

While this doesn't fit the picture of surrounding yourself with loved ones on your wedding day, think about what else is missing—the whining, the arguments, the refusal to wear yellow, the hurt feelings (yours and your errant bridesmaids'), and the resulting long-term animosity. Now think about what's left: You, your fiancé, an officiant, and a witness or two . . . oh, and marital bliss.

Chapter 3

Financial Considerations

Are you having a hard time justifying spending all that money on *one day* out of your entire life? You're in good company. Many couples today are refusing to go into debt for wedding expenses. Is there really a way to keep some of your money and come out on the other side happily married? You bet there is. If your budget has been on your mind lately, perhaps eloping is the right decision for you.

A Word on Budgeting

Time was, Dear Old Dad opened up his checkbook and took care of the wedding finances for the young bride, but times have changed. These days, many couples are spending their own hard-earned money to pay for their wedding. Now, considering the fact that many couples marry in their twenties and early thirties, it's safe to say that most of them are not independently wealthy by the time they walk down the aisle.

 FACT

> A couple who is considering the Big Wedding with an eye on their modest budget is quickly going to come to the conclusion that this event is going to put their finances into disarray. If you and your groom are going to lose sleep over paying for the centerpieces at a huge reception, eloping might be a better option.

These are couples on a budget, couples who have to make *choices*. Should we have two smaller car payments and two average cars, or one big payment and share the luxury coupe? Should we buy the less expensive mac and cheese, or should we splurge on the filet mignon? Should we turn the lights on tonight so we can see each other or should we leave them off and save money? Should we spend every single penny we have on our wedding or should we be a little more frugal?

Fortunately, being forced to budget from the get-go has its benefits. Couples who are stringent about their finances learn to live with the attitude of, "If we can't afford it, we can't afford it," no ands, ifs, or buts. These are the couples who are going to make the wisest decisions about spending their money—and that includes their wedding expenses.

He Just Hired a Helicopter Limo!

So here you go, into a marriage with a spender— problem is, neither of you has much to spend. He's planning a wedding blowout, something no one else will ever come close to matching. He's still cackling to himself about his latest ingenious plan: He's going to hire a fleet of helicopters to whisk you and the guests off to a mountaintop reception. It's just amazing what you can put on a credit card.

If eloping is on your mind strictly because it makes the most economic sense, you're going to need backup in the form of bank statements and your current bills to convince your spendaholic man. Yelling and crying aren't going to get you far with your Mr. Moneybags, because he'll think you're overreacting. Be rational. Don't fight. Present the facts as they are. Offer an alternative—one that you can afford. A little trip to that wedding chapel and a nice weekend in the country might start sounding pretty nice to him once reality hits him in the head.

ⓔ ALERT!

Before he ruins you completely, grab your scissors and destroy his plastic. This man needs a little lesson in finances, and you might want to start with the basics. Sometimes a little kick in the pants will wake him up to the reality that you are going to have to actually pay for his eccentric tastes one of these days.

But It's My Wedding!

Ah ha! So *you're* the troublemaker. Well, you're right; it is your wedding—or, rather, it's half yours. You're about to start a life with this man you love. The word *compromise* should work its way into your vocabulary right about now.

If you're dead set on the Big Wedding and he's dead set against it (because he's frugal), meet in the middle. Perhaps, and it's just a thought, you can spend top dollar on your elopement. You'll be hard-pressed finding a way to spend tens of thousands of dollars on a short marriage getaway (which isn't to say it can't be done, so watch yourself). And maybe, just maybe, your future husband won't object so strongly to spending that money on yourselves instead of on dinner for 300 acquaintances.

Talking Turkey—and All the Rest

Face it—a wedding can leave almost any couple in the poor house. It's just too easy to lose control and start spending money you don't have and may never earn in your lifetime on pricey caterers, handcrafted wedding shoes, and the hottest band in town. And it doesn't help that the entire wedding industry promotes $25,000-plus weddings as the norm. Is it wrong *not* to spend tens of thousands of dollars on your wedding? Will your marriage be off to a rocky start if you don't throw your bouquet to a crowd of several hundred women? The answer, in succinct form, is "no."

Snowballing Spending

No matter what kind of deals you try to finagle, you're not going to escape the Big Wedding unscathed. Even if you do find a dress at a rock-bottom price (still at several hundreds of dollars), it's very unlikely that you're going to get a good price on everything else associated with setting up the big day.

Once you enter the wedding industry world, money becomes an expendable commodity. Even if you're normally very careful about your spending, you still may find yourself paying $85 for that strapless bra marketed specifically for the bride-to-be, because you've already spent so much money on every other wedding detail that $85 seems like a drop in the hat.

Eloping, conversely, tends to ground you a little more in reality. Yes, you're getting married, and yes, it's very exciting—but you *know* you're not going to hire a professional makeup artist to make you look gorgeous for your sunset vows on a mountaintop. Couples who elope are often able to avoid these errors in financial judgment precisely because they don't *want* the extras; it's one of the reasons they chose to elope in the first place.

Is a Celebrity Wedding Right for You?

Weddings today are getting bigger and gaudier, more expensive, and far less personal. Take the time to ask yourself where brides are getting the idea that bigger is better—and that huge is best. Perhaps they've been to one too many of those weddings, but how did the Outrageously Huge Wedding dig its claws into mainstream America?

 FACT

A wedding displayed on the pages of your favorite magazine is affordable for celebrities, partly because they're regularly inundated with gifts, like the bridal party's wildly expensive trinkets, in exchange for the free advertising for the supplier. You, on the other hand, are going to have to pay retail.

The media may be the culprit. Every magazine and TV show has a Celebrity Weddings edition that includes advice on how to replicate this wedding for you and your fiancé. And there's no doubt about it—these weddings are beautiful. If they weren't, they wouldn't be featured so prominently, but ask yourself some critical questions:

1. Why would anyone invite the media to a wedding?
2. Do you really expect the same reaction to your own huge, overpriced wedding?
3. Are you willing to spend every cent you have to feel like a media celebrity for twenty-four hours?

The answer to the first question is complex. The media are invited for several reasons. First of all, celebrities need the press. And celebrity weddings are all about advertising. Think about it. As your own wedding approaches, you'll take a greater interest in who designed the bride's dress, whose name is on the groom's tux, and whether or not a major department store—one with a branch in your own town—provided the gifts for the bridesmaids. Now, do you see where this is going?

If you fall for this marketing ploy, you are not going to be a celebrity when it's over. Even if you score the biggest picture on the Society Page, you're still going to be left with a stack of wedding bills.

So, in summary: The famous wedding couple gets a bunch of freebees, the designers are going to sell more dresses at an incredible markup, and the publisher is going to sell a lot of magazines. Meanwhile, *you're* going to pay top dollar to duplicate a celebrity wedding just to prove . . . what? That you're capable of being as beautiful as a movie star on your wedding day?

The beaded dress isn't going to give you that glow—standing at an altar with your honey is. And that actress? She's glowing because this wedding layout is going to revive her faltering career.

Eloping focuses on what *you* want, not what the wedding industry wants to sell you as the norm. What's more personal than pledging your life to someone forever? You don't need the crowd, the designer dress, or a picture of yourself in the local paper. Let someone else have all of that—namely, the women who make their livings off of their images.

Your Economic Status

The first thing you should consider when planning your wedding budget is your situation. You may feel as though you're doing fine, but before you start spending your hard-earned cash on a lavish wedding, ask yourself if you can really, truly afford it. Couples who are "doing fine" often wish to remain on the course instead of taking a detour on the Wedding Debt Highway.

Are You Independently Wealthy?

There are some brides out there who really can afford the great big wedding with all the trimmings. They don't need to skimp on one single thing. They can serve prime rib at the reception *and* wear the incredibly costly bridal ensemble. They can purchase the best gifts for the bridal party *and* still afford a month abroad in the most spectacular hotels for their honeymoon.

On an Average Budget

If you aren't independently wealthy, you may fall into the category most engaged women find themselves in— you're of average means looking at above-average wedding expenditures. There's nothing wrong with that if your heart is in it, but what if it isn't? What if you're feeling torn on the subject, as though you'd like to just turn your back on all of the planning and expense?

You can, in fact, turn your back on it, and you won't be alone. As wedding costs continue to increase, there seems to be a trend toward common sense—a backlash against going into debt in order to pay for a big reception and an ornate dress. Couples are intelligently looking for more reasonable wedding alternatives.

ⒺQUESTION?

But what if I'm well-off financially? Should I still be concerned about the cost of the Big Wedding?

Even if you're a well-off bride, it doesn't mean you have to spend all that money on your wedding. Remember, your wedding is not about appearances. If you're not comfortable with the Big Wedding setup, don't do it. Following your own instincts is the biggest statement you can make.

Don't worry about what anyone else is going to think about your elopement. This wedding is going to affect *your* economic future. Your marriage is either going to start out on firm financial footing (if you plan your wedding responsibly) or on a slippery slope (when you realize just how much of the Big Wedding expenses you charged on your various credit cards).

 **ALERT!**

The truth of the matter is, everyone who has a Big Wedding either spends a heap of cash on it or goes into debt to pay for it. Could this be the reason why your heart isn't in the whole scene? Consider yourself wise beyond your years.

Start Off on the Right Foot

Money is the root of countless arguments in many relationships. If you and your future husband are at odds over how much you're willing to go into debt to pay for this wedding—or about how much of your savings should go toward your veil—this is *not* an argument that's going to disappear after you're wed. If one of you spends every last dime on that Big Wedding against the other's wishes, and there's nothing left to pay the rent with *after* the wedding, what do you think is going to happen? Two words: Big Trouble.

Real Life? Real Expensive

The fact is that life is expensive. If you're just going through the motions of having a traditional wedding to please your family, or because you think it will be kind of a fun thing to do, think again, especially if you're normally the frugal type who balks at paying large sums of money on frivolous items.

If you refuse to pay retail for anything, opting to wait for a sale instead, it doesn't make sense for you to blow a ton of money now on the Mother of All Weddings. Elopements are like finding the one skirt in your size on the sale rack in the back corner of your favorite store. It's like it was made for you, and you love it all the more because you didn't spend your whole paycheck on it.

In the end, if you put your wedding money toward your *marriage*, you'll have something to feel good about every single day for years to come.

Rainy Days

Even if you're not necessarily concerned about going into some wedding debt, you shouldn't set yourself up for what could be a serious cash flow problem. You don't want to spend every last dime you have on your wedding, thinking that you're so young, you'll pay it off before you're thirty (or thirty-five, or forty). Putting all your eggs into one basket, even if the basket is covered in lace and silk, is never a good idea.

Remember: Cars break down. Spouses get laid off. The dog gets sick. Kids come along when you least expect them. These are the things you need to have some money set aside for, just in case.

 FACT

> You can't plan for everything, but you should have a prudent financial plan for emergencies, especially after you're married. It makes getting through a financial crisis so much easier on your marriage if you're not literally forced into looking for change in the sofa to pay for food.

And if you're already strapped for cash, you're even more vulnerable to life's curveballs. If you spend everything you have (and a lot of what you don't have) on a huge wedding and some huge life crisis does pop up months later, your young marriage will be in for a test that many long-term unions have difficulty surviving.

Plan for a Big Future

Instead of planning the Big Wedding, why not plan big for your marriage. Just think of all the vast options for spending your money:

- A down payment on a house
- A new car
- Getting rid of the debt you already have
- Financial investments for the future

You may be amazed at how long it can take to save your money for the items on this seemingly small list, but there's no time like the present.

The House

Does it seem as though everyone you know has given up their city lives and moved out to the 'burbs? Or maybe they've stayed in the city but they moved into a gorgeous restored Victorian in the old part of town. Right about now, you're looking from your checkbook balance to the wedding magazine to your flow sheet of Big Wedding expenses, and you're thinking, "I'm going to be living in this tiny apartment for the next fifty years."

Nothing wrong with that, if that's what you want. But if you're thinking you're ready to spread your wings a little, a house is probably on your list of purchases in the not-too-distant future.

No matter how you slice it, buying a home is going to cost you big bucks. The best way to do it is to have some money saved for all of these expenses, so that when the furnace goes, you won't have to start burning your wedding gifts to heat your pad.

If you're willing to give up the Big Wedding for something more permanent, move the wedding funds into the House Account. You will have traded a fleeting moment for a physical structure, not to mention an investment in the future. Instead of lining your landlord's pockets, you're paying into your home's equity—and there'll be a huge payoff for you in the future.

The Car

If you live in a booming metropolis and the transit system is first-rate, consider yourself very lucky. If, however, you're living in a town where the busses seem to appear at will and there's no train to speak of, you're probably going to need a dependable car to get yourself back and forth to work at some point.

Here's the clincher with autos: Car repair bills are like utility bills (which, by the way, are another huge expense)—no one can justify that huge amount for a plastic piece of a pulley, and for all you know, it might have only cost the garage fifty cents. You're pretty much at the mercy of the powers that be in this situation, especially when your car won't run without that little expensive doohickey.

Ⓔ ESSENTIAL

Why incur even more debt by throwing a three-ring wedding? It doesn't make good economic sense, especially if you're already in debt. Opting for a smaller, cheaper ceremony is a smart move when you're faced with mounds of bills stretching decades into the future.

In addition, you'll have insurance, gas, and routine maintenance to pay for—and it all adds up fast. Counting your quarters to see how much gas you can afford is no fun, and if you opt to spend your life's savings on a big, fancy wedding ceremony, you might start to wonder if that money would have been better spent on the rest of your life.

Getting Out of Your Debtor's Prison

All right, it's not that bad. You're not sitting in a cell until you pay off your student loans, but it can definitely feel that way when you're faced with an entry-level salary, a tight budget, and a positively huge monthly payment to the lender—your way of thanking them for your education. Or maybe you've gotten in over your head with your credit cards, which is not hard to do in this cashless world we're living in today.

Financial Investments

You want to see your money grow? You want to retire by the time you're fifty? You're thinking practically, which is great. You'll need a good financial advisor. Oh, and you'll need some dough, too. (As good as your advisor is, she can't do a thing with your wink and smile.)

Shifting that money from Wedding Fund to Retirement Fund will put you on the fast track to where you want to be in thirty years, and you'll be patting yourself on the back when you get there as you and your husband are looking at your elopement pictures and saying, "You know, we did the right thing."

It's Your Money, So Keep It

It's a common misconception that bigger is better. However, the *least* advantageous way to spend your money, from a practical standpoint, is on a huge wedding. Even if you don't have your sights set on a celebrity wedding, there'll be a lot of expenses to handle: dressmakers, reception halls, limousine companies, and cake shops will all need to be paid.

Think of it in these terms: If you saw a friend struggling to make ends meet—paying off her student loans, making a huge car payment every month, scrounging to pay her rent—and you saw that she was charging up a storm on her credit cards buying lots of little pastries and a frilly dress that she's going to wear just once, you'd say something, right?

Consider some other ways to blow big money on your Big Wedding:

- Appetizers for 400 guests
- Dinner for the same people who just pigged out on the expensive appetizers
- An open bar for these truly gluttonous people
- Wedding cake
- A separate dessert because no one likes wedding cake
- Pastry trays for later in the evening—when everyone is hungry again

And that's just the food portion of your wedding expenses. In addition to paying a bundle to feed near-strangers, you're also going to end up with a very expensive dress that you will never wear again, shoes that match the dress, and a stack of bills you will not believe. Not a financially sound plan, when you could have a much smaller affair and be just as married at the end of it.

No Frills Necessary

When you opt to elope, you're basically saying, "We don't need all the bells and whistles to feel married." That includes dispensing with transportation for your proposed wedding party of twenty, fresh floral center-pieces, the DJ or band, a towering cake, the flowers for the bridesmaids, tuxedos, dresses, the overpriced (and temperamental) photographer, the rehearsal dinner, the reception, the open bar at the reception, the right table linens—the list is endless.

Ⓔ ESSENTIAL

If you're feeling unsure about spending $1,000 on a wedding cake or fancy flowers, that says a lot about you—that you're practical and not swayed by the pretty pictures in the magazines, that you're grounded in the real world and you want to start your married life off on firm financial footing. Hooray for you!

Tally up what you're going to save. Take heed: You will not trust your math at first. After a nervous fit of laughter, realizing how you've narrowly escaped the wedding gauntlet, you will ask yourself and anyone who crosses your path, "Do you know what lilies of the valley cost out of season?! And they're only *in* season for two weeks of the year! How does anyone know that expensive wedding cake *isn't* a mix from a box?! Why would anyone pay these exorbitant prices? It's a travesty!"

The point is, cutting out the extras is amazingly easy to do once you start analyzing the final costs, and almost everything involved with a Big Wedding is extra. After you add up how much you're going to spend on the tiniest details, it's not so hard to convince yourself that you should find a way to get married *and* keep some of your cash. Eloping is one of the best ways to kill these two birds with one stone.

Better Ways to Spend the Dough

All that money you save by skipping the Big Wedding may go toward a better elopement experience. Your overnight stay in a bed-and-breakfast can be extended to a weeklong sojourn. Or maybe—just maybe—your budget allows you to stretch it into a tropical excursion. Put the options on your mental scale: Big Wedding or big, long vacation? Which one is tipping the balance?

With the Big Wedding plans in the works, you may not have enough money left over for a decent honeymoon. Sure, you can opt to start saving up after the Big Wedding and take the honeymoon when you can afford it, but you're only going to be newlyweds for a short time. Like it or not, it's going to have a different feel if you have to put it on hold for a year. By that time, you will be well acquainted with your honey as a husband—husbandly quirks and all.

Chapter 4

Reasons to Reconsider

By now, you're probably convinced that elopement is the way to go. You're ready to pick a place and head off in that direction with your groom in tow. But before you start making plans, take another moment to think about it. Do you feel excited about eloping— or just sick of making wedding plans? Have you shared your elopement plans with at least one friend? Before you make your final decision, you need to review some not-so-good reasons for eloping.

Marry Me Now—or Never

It's one thing to elope because you reject the idea of having the Big Wedding. It's an entirely different thing to elope because you're rushing into a marriage you're not entirely certain is right for you. Sometimes it just wasn't meant to be. If you're thinking of getting married just because you feel like you're at the age where you should, or if you're afraid that your relationship won't survive a lengthy separation without wedding vows, perhaps it's time to think again.

Together Forever—Already

If you've ever had a long-term boyfriend, you know how it feels to ask yourself, "What are we doing together at this point? We're past the lovey-dovey stage of dating. We've been together six years. Where is this relationship going?"

 FACT

Settling for marriage just because you've been dating or living with someone for years isn't a good enough reason to pledge your entire life to that person. There has to be more—like that you actually want to be with this guy forever. That's a good starting point.

These are valid questions, and they should be answered over a series of long talks with the boyfriend, not with a spur-of-the-moment retreat to a wedding chapel. There may be a reason you're not married at this point. Maybe the two of you want very different things out of life. Maybe one of you really doesn't want to be married, but feels that it's bizarre *not* to marry the person you've been with for a big part of your adult life. Maybe you've only been together this long because it's been easy—a lot easier than a messy breakup and moving on into the unknown. This may be the case especially if you've been living together. Your lives are, for all intents and purposes, joined together anyway. Of course, right now you can walk away without a lot of legal hassles.

What's the Rush?

There are many other reasons you might want to marry him as soon as possible:

- You have a baby on the way.
- He's been getting friendly with a girl in his office.
- Your family is pressuring you.
- You're tired of introducing him as your "boyfriend," and you won't introduce him as your "live-in lover."
- It's just time.

Look at this list. What's missing? How about love? Eloping may be a temporary bucket of water on the stress fires that are raging in your relationship, but eventually it will come down to this: Do you really want to be together? Are the two of you able to make this work, and work *well*?

If you feel like you could take him or leave him—but he's still hanging around, so you might as well take him—give yourself more time to consider if this is really what you want.

Eloping on Military Time

Is there anything more heartbreaking than the sight of a military man leaving his girl behind? Not really. There he goes, waving as his ship pulls away, and you're left on the pier wishing that you had tied the knot before he left. The perfect bookend to this scene is when he comes home. It may seem like the perfect scene for eloping, but there's a realistic side that you must consider first.

Ⓔ ALERT!

Military couples sometimes choose to elope because the enlisted partner's paycheck is sometimes increased to allow for supporting a spouse. Bad thinking. Money alone can't make a relationship into marriage material.

He's Shipping Out

The thing about marrying a military man is that it's not just a long-distance relationship. He's not off working in an office somewhere, able to hop on a plane and see you for the weekend. His workplace is sometimes a battlefield, or at the very least, a training ground. The government owns him. He can't come running back to you when you need him (or when your child is born), he can't always be reached so that you can hear his voice, and he may be in danger—it's the nature of his job. He can be called to defend the country at any time.

Military marriages suffer from many pressures (long absences, tight budgets, constant relocation). Some couples are able to handle it; many others aren't. When you're young and in love and he's shipping out, it's all very dramatic and sad. When you're left all alone, it can be even worse.

Sara saw a lot of broken military marriages when she lived on a naval base with her husband. Many of those marriages were the result of last-minute elopements just before the men were shipping out for months on end. "You could just see it coming with some of these couples," says Sara. "They were young and in love, and they were in a rush to get married. A lot of the girls were just too young to realize what they were getting into. They still had a lot of growing up to do. After their husbands shipped out, we'd see a lot of these girls in the bars, hooking up with guys from the town.

"I would say *most* of those 'quickie' marriages didn't last. It wasn't unusual to hear about a marriage breaking up after a year or two. And a lot of the marriages that *did* last longer than that probably shouldn't have."

Is the moral of this story that one should never marry a mate who is in the armed forces? Of course not. The message is to be careful: Don't rush into eloping, especially if you're still very young and your potential husband is leaving on the next submarine. As romantic as eloping with your man in uniform sounds, remember that most couples come back from their elopement to establish a household together. Are you both committed and mature enough to handle long separations? If you have any doubts, wait until you're absolutely sure.

He's Coming Home!

Let's say you have a military boyfriend who's been gone for several months. You've been dating for a while, so you know him well, and you know you want to marry him—there's not a doubt in your mind. You're going to meet him at the airport when his plane comes in, and you're going to drive straight to city hall and get hitched!

Slow down for just a minute. You're excited that he's coming back to you—of course you are. But he's been gone a long time. At the very least, give yourselves a little time to get used to being around each other again and to make sure that the flame didn't burn out while he was away. The last thing you want is to find out a week after your elopement that he's changed a lot, or that you have.

If you were talking about tying the knot before he left, take the time to make sure that this relationship is still on the marriage track. Distance can make the heart grow fonder, but sometimes putting miles between the two of you just makes you feel . . . distant. Eloping shouldn't be about reclaiming your territory. It should be about starting a new life together. Make sure you both still want the same thing before you head off to the wedding chapel.

It's a Matter of Trust

You don't trust him with the new secretary, and you think the ring will help? Think again. That's definitely another bad reason to marry someone. If there's no trust before you marry, what makes you think there'll be trust afterward? A piece of paper with your names on it does not guarantee fidelity.

Ⓔ ESSENTIAL

If he's going to break off your relationship because he thinks you're unfaithful and/or you don't love him and marrying him is the only way to prove that you're actually as solid as a rock, let him go. That's one marriage you definitely don't want to be a part of.

If your boyfriend thinks that eloping will prove to him that you are faithful, you're headed for a marriage that's full of trouble. Guess what's going to happen after you sign the marriage license? He still won't trust you, and you'll be expected to prove everything now, because you've set a precedent—you're willing to take extraordinary measures to prove your love to him.

Claiming Your Man

This is a situation a plain Jane can often find herself in: After years of dating really boring guys, you've finally found someone who rocks your world. He's a hottie, he's incredibly fun, and your girlfriends are very jealous. He's perfect—but those girlfriends are getting a little too close for comfort, and come to think of it, so are a bunch of other women. And your hunk does very little to discourage the attention.

What do you do? You suggest a weekend getaway in his favorite place, Las Vegas! Your treat, of course—as long as you stop at that drive-through wedding chapel place real quick.

 FACT

It's very easy to confuse lust and infatuation and excitement with love—especially if you've never dated anyone like your current man before. Don't sweat it. A wild and crazy relationship can be a lot of fun, as long as you don't rush into a marriage you really didn't want.

Deep down, you know this isn't the way to get your man. A guy who's living his life on display is fun to be with, but is that the only reason you want him? Sure, he's going to make a great trophy for you, but do you realize the price you're going to pay? You're going to be cleaning up after this man and doing his laundry, making his lunches and listening to him snore. Are you in love with him enough to tolerate all of this, or is it just his pretty face you like?

Nothing is more disappointing in life than realizing that the hot guy you *think* you're in love with—and who seems to be really into you right now—is, indeed, a human being after all. He has his faults. He's kind of shallow, it's *really* hard to have an intelligent conversation with him, and he seems to really like the ladies a lot. In fact, his looks and bad-boy attitude are just about all he has going for him.

He is a major coup for you—which is exactly *why* you want him—but you don't really, truly love him. Don't make the mistake of luring him into your life for keeps. You may find you're completely incompatible. He may make a better memory than a husband.

Family Troubles

When you're faced with your family's hatred for your boyfriend, life can be a miserable thing. You want to be with him, and your mom goes out of her way to make sure you aren't. Suddenly, she's planning out your days and leaving you no free time, or she's commenting on your plans every time you walk out the door. Or is it that your boyfriend dislikes your family? He wants you all to himself and won't try to see your dad's point that your family does want to see you once in a while, especially since you do live in the same town. How can you make peace between these fighting factions? *Not* by eloping, that's for sure.

You're Not Sixteen Anymore

Rebellion is a funny thing. Suddenly, you love everything your parents hate, just because they hate it. Or you hate what they love. Make no mistake: Rebellion can rear its nasty little head at any age. You don't have to be a teenager to be caught in the act of rolling your eyes and doing the complete opposite of what your parents have suggested. The problem is, rebellion can drive you to do things that you don't even want to do—just to prove you can.

While buying a fire engine red car or dying your hair blue or getting a big old tattoo may drive your parents mad, marrying a guy they hate just to stick it to them is going to hurt *you* the most in the long run. Your parents may very well get over it, either by forgiving you or giving up on you, but you will be stuck in the marriage.

Ⓔ ALERT!

If you've married him just to make your family mad, there's no way to tell if you loved him in the first place. Marriages based on defiance have a rocky road ahead of them.

Dealing with a Mama's Boy

On the flip side, maybe you're the one that his family does not approve of. You know you're a nice person, you know that you really love him, and you just can't for the life of you understand why they're against your marrying their boy. You're the best thing that's ever happened to him.

You both want to get married, and it seems best to avoid his family by eloping. However, learning that you've lured their son away to trap him into marrying you (which is exactly what they'll think happened) isn't going to make his family accept you any faster. In fact, it may make things about 100 times worse. Also, is it possible that your *beau* is the one in the throes of rebellion? What could be worse than being described as the wife he married because he was trying to make his mother angry? Ask yourself the following questions:

- Is there an old girlfriend his mother loved, and you're the complete opposite of her?
- Does he only pay close attention to you in front of his family?
- Is everything a competition in his family?
- Does he enjoy pushing other people's buttons?
- Is he the black sheep of his family—always trying to prove he's different?
- Did the marriage topic come up out of the blue—much to your surprise?

If you answered yes to any of these questions, you may want to take a step back. You don't want to end up a pawn in a family squabble. Try to work things out with the family before you plan any type of wedding. It will make your life much easier. If they're completely unreasonable, that's a different story all together—but if they seem like sane people on every issue except this one, or if things were fine between you and his mom until the subject of marriage came up, maybe they're seeing something you don't.

Do They Have a Point?

When you're in love, it's hard to admit that your boyfriend (or fiancé) has faults. But if the flaws are there, they're not going to improve after you start wearing a wedding band. If your family is dead set against you marrying a certain someone, don't go flying off the handle, assuming they want to ruin your life. Chances are, they have your best interests at heart.

Take a good, honest look at your relationship. Are there fundamental differences between the two of you? Is he using your credit cards to party all day while you slave away at the office everyday? Does he want eight kids and a farm while you are bound and determined to remain childless and stay in the city? Is he jealous or violent?

It's difficult—and often impossible—to see the fault lines in a relationship when you're in it. If you family is voicing their concerns, listen to them. They may not be right, but give them the floor to address their worries. Maybe it's all a misunderstanding—a long talk may clear up things for everyone concerned.

I Just Want to Be a Bride

Here comes the bride, and she's not even looking at the groom. She's late because she was just dazzled by her reflection in the mirror. And here's another one, who's so happy to be finally getting married; she spent the last six months fretting because she's turning thirty-five next year and she *has* to be married by then. Are you getting the feeling that something is wrong here?

 FACT

> While getting married is fun, it is also a very serious step in your life. You should have some idea of who your fiancé is before you take your vows. Otherwise, it will come as a shock to realize that you've married a virtual stranger because he looked like the dream guy you always thought you'd marry.

It's Not Play Pretend

You know the type. This woman thinks that getting married is fun. In fact, she used to play Bride as a child and planned out her wedding in great detail by the time she turned fifteen. All she's ever talked about is being a Mrs., but Mrs. who? Are you getting the feeling that the surname doesn't really make a difference at this point? Let's hope that this bride isn't you.

Sure, many little girls dream of being a bride. They imagine the man who will come and sweep them off their feet, take them off to a beautiful home, a man who will take care of them, and so on. But in those dreams, the man doesn't seem to have a face or any defining characteristics, like a sense of humor or a moral conviction. That doesn't matter. He just needs to be the husband. The rest will all work itself out.

At least it will in the little game of House that you played way back when. This isn't the right way to pick out a real hubby. The excitement of being married wears off, and then you need to have something else to rely on, like the fact that he makes you laugh, or that you love his mind. He needs to be more than a two-dimensional figure in your life.

If you're planning your elopement and the only thing you're really dreaming about is the trip itself, or how everyone will react when you return ("They'll be so happy for me! I mean, they'll be so happy for us!"), or how good you're going to look in those wedding pictures on the beach, ask yourself where the groom fits in to all of this. Is he just a prop?

Ⓔ ALERT!

Don't grab the first guy who seems willing to elope just because he's an easy mark. You both deserve better than that, and in the end, when you do find the perfect guy, you'll be glad you're not married to someone who's less than ideal.

Eek! Look at the Year!

Unfortunately, a common source of anxiety among women who are ready to get married is their age. Many women have it in their minds that they have to be married by the time they reach a certain chronological number or they will never experience marital bliss.

If you're having these thoughts, remind yourself that you're in luck—it's the twenty-first century. The belief that there's some kind of a marriage deadline is an antiquated myth. Even back in the days when unmarried women were cruelly referred to as Old Maids, there were those who married late in life. You're fortunate enough to be living in a day and age where marriage isn't a woman's crowning achievement.

(E) ESSENTIAL

Brides who are focused on finding the right man are going to choose well, because they're more mature and have an idea of what marriage is really all about. Don't risk becoming a divorce statistic merely because you didn't want to face another year alone. Your payoff for waiting may be huge.

If you're packing your bags for an elopement trip and the only thing you see circled on your calendar is your upcoming deadline, stop. This is another example of settling for a certain marriage because of a fabricated situation. Make sure you *love* this guy, and that he's not just fulfilling a compulsion for you.

It may well be that things have worked out coincidentally—you wanted to be married by the time you were thirty-three, and two months before your birthday, the perfect man walked into your life. That can happen. But because you have already set a goal for yourself, you need to be on your guard and make sure you've chosen him because of who he is, not because of how old you are.

Not Without My Family

Getting married without your family—it may sound like a dream to some brides, but to others it's simply unimaginable. If the thought of saying, "I do" without your mom or your sisters or your best friend standing right behind you sends you into a deep depression, it doesn't have to. Eloping carries the connotation of being some big, secret affair, but it doesn't have to be. There are *very* few rules about eloping, so you can make them up as you see fit.

If circumstances permit, you can invite your immediate family to your elopement. If you think your mother is going to freak out over your inviting her to a Las Vegas wedding chapel, then obviously you shouldn't. But if you think your family will understand why you don't want the Big Wedding, and you don't think your mom will issue one of her ultimatums ("If you elope, you are not welcome in my house!"), go ahead and let them in on your plans. Maybe you can have everything you want—a hassle-free getaway wedding with your family there to wish you well.

Mom's Going to Be So Mad

Families can be such complicated groupings. You love each other, and yet no one can push your buttons like your closest relatives. They may misunderstand your intentions, or it may be that you don't give them a chance to hear them out on certain issues.

Ⓔ **ALERT!**

> Eloping *doesn't* mean that you don't love your family, no matter what they say. But if what they say means a great deal to you, it may be wise to reconsider.

Before you elope, make sure you can accept the worst-case scenario of your family's reaction. If you know there's no way you can stand to be at odds with your family, and you know they're never going to accept an elopement (even though it's the kind of wedding you really want), you have to think very long and hard about your options. The family drama resulting from your elopement could drive a wedge between you and your new husband. He may not understand why you're so sad when you're a newlywed, which would defeat the entire point of your being together in the first place.

So What's Your Final Answer?

It's time to make your decision. Are you absolutely sure you want to choose elopement? It's one thing to dismiss the Big Wedding in the name of romance, but can you really withstand the assault from the wedding industry that will follow you ever after? You're not going to be one of those brides with regrets about her wedding, are you? It's best to give yourself some time to evaluate what you really want and need. If all goes as planned, you'll only get to do this once.

You will not ever get another chance to wear a big taffeta and silk hand-beaded white wedding dress. Even if—and this is the greatest of ifs—you end up marrying again, big white wedding dresses are traditionally for first-time brides. If tears are welling up in your eyes every time you think about walking down the aisle in a simpler outfit, this may be a sign of a larger issue. Maybe you do want the Big Wedding after all.

Chapter 5
Get Cracking!

Congratulations—you've made up your mind and are ready to go. Will you plan a getaway or take off on a moment's notice? Where are you headed and where will you stay? What will you and your fiancé wear? Just because you've chosen to elope, it doesn't mean you must leave everything to chance. If you want to find just the right dress or prepare your own vows, it's time to get cracking! Do some research and make some basic arrangement for an elopement you'll never forget.

A Planned Elopement

Sure, when most people hear the word *elopement,* they think of last-minute trips to the local justice of the peace. That's one way to do it. However, you're not limited to staying local, or to keeping things simple. These days, many couples plan their elopements well in advance of the actual date. Some couples are looking for the best deal; others are just too busy to run off this weekend and get married; still others have very unique ideas and they need some time to pull everything together.

Ⓔ ESSENTIAL

Don't think of planning an elopement as cutting down on the romance factor. The real romance lies in the fact that the two of you want to be together forever and will go to any lengths to make that happen.

Whittling Down the Possibilities

Some couples choose to elope in style—complete with fancy wedding clothes, a classy setting, and a gourmet meal to celebrate their union. Other couples choose to be more spontaneous; they opt for a minimal amount of planning and let fate take the wheel. Chapter 6 discusses some popular elopement destinations, but before you can decide *where* to go, you need to figure out what kind of elopement you're looking for.

You Need Hustle and Bustle

You're a little on the wild side, you don't care much for tradition, and you're looking to have a fun time before *and* after you say your vows. Look for a place that offers lots of action and excitement—Las Vegas, New York City, Chicago, Miami, or any big city. Another option is a resort area, but make sure you choose the right one. Some resorts are geared toward total relaxation, which could be a real bummer if you're looking to dance your nights away.

 **ALERT!**

What you don't want to do is pick a place that doesn't fit your needs. The brochure from the private island may look like paradise—no cars, no bars, no shopping—but if you know the quiet will drive you batty, look elsewhere.

You may end up being bored to tears on your honeymoon, which may lead you to think that your new husband is the problem—when, in fact, if you two were in your natural habitat (the concrete jungle), you'd be having a swinging time. When you're counting the days until you can return to civilization, you'll wish you had chosen a more populated spot.

You Crave Quiet Romance

Does a week of complete quiet sound like the type of elopement you're looking for? This is exactly what some couples dream about—time together with nothing to do but talk, hold hands, and revel in your newlywed status.

The exact opposite advice holds true for you, then. Assuming you have the time to plan a getaway, look for a quiet spot. It doesn't necessarily have to be an island. It can be a sleepy little town with a justice of the peace. What you should try to avoid, however, is a city that doesn't sleep. You may find yourself trying to stare into each other's eyes while trying to ignore the *thumpa-thumpa-thump* from the disco next door to your hotel, or the nonstop sirens whizzing by.

If you and your fiancé are both on the mellower side—nightclubs aren't really your thing and crowds make you claustrophobic *and* highly irritable—look for an elopement spot that offers peace and quiet. You don't have to be able to afford an exclusive spot; you just need to do your research.

 FACT

> You can ask a travel agent for some guidance on the right destination for you. And if you have a spot in mind, call the local city hall. They'll be able to give you information on their justice of the peace and they can hook you up with the local visitor's bureau, just in case you do want to get outside your hotel room once in a while.

Let's Just Do It!

Maybe you don't have time to call around and talk to 100 different people about your elopement plans. Maybe you just want to get going and get married—to heck with the rest of it. You don't plan anything, and that's the way you like it. Too much planning leads to ultimate disappointment, so you avoid plans altogether.

You may be in luck just by living in your particular state. While just over half of the fifty states have a waiting period between obtaining the marriage license and becoming man and wife, just *under* half of them have no waiting period at all.

Ⓔ ESSENTIAL

To find out if your state has a waiting period and how long that waiting period is, check out the Web sites listed in Appendix A, or pick up your phone book and call your city or town hall. They have all the information.

Getting Creative

Unlike a traditional wedding, eloping is completely personal, so if the mood strikes you, take it in any direction you like—get creative. If city hall isn't your thing, you can get married just about anywhere else. It's up to you to do the research and hammer out all the details. As you'll soon discover, there are some very unusual options available to you.

Outdoor Weddings

You are not limited to a church and a ballroom. You're not held to a chapel or a restaurant. If you love the woods, put on your hiking shoes and clear out an altar. What could be more perfect for a pair of nature lovers than reciting your vows as you stand under a canopy of trees, inhaling the scent of fresh air around you and listening to the sounds of the forest as you become man and wife?

Beach weddings are also a popular option with eloping couples. Just imagine: You'll stand at the ocean's edge, listening to the waves lap at the shore, smelling the salt air, feeling the breeze on your skin, and watching the sun set as you marry the man of your dreams.

Ⓔ ESSENTIAL

If the sunset is your thing but the beach isn't, you can plan a dusk wedding inland. Picture this: You and your fiancé in an outdoor garden surrounded by beautiful lanterns. Or maybe a gazebo is more your style, or perhaps even the deck in your own parklike backyard, glowing with candlelight. It would be *so* romantic.

Hitting the Slopes

So you love to spend your weekends skiing, and you want to squeeze a little ceremony in, too? Check out some of the ski resorts out West. Many have elopement packages specifically designed for ski bunnies like you—and some friends, if you so desire.

Another bonus for eloping skiers: In Colorado, the marriage laws allow you to marry yourselves, no officiant necessary. You will have to obtain the marriage license first (no skimping on the details, here—you want everything to be *legal* in the end), take the lift up the mountain, recite your own vows, and arrive at the bottom of the slopes as Mr. and Mrs.

Don't Limit Yourself

The beauty of eloping is that you're not restricted by any wedding rules. You can get as creative and outlandish as you want. Remember, you don't have to explain any of your plans to guests or parents who would no doubt frown on some of the following ideas. Consider these spots for celebrating your elopement:

The links. Are you a confirmed golf nut? Arrange to have your minister meet you at the first tee. (You'll also need to clear it with the golf course—most likely, you'll have to move *away* from the tee to let others play through while you say, "I do.") Take your new husband and play eighteen holes. And you don't have to let him win.

Submerged. Have you always wanted to scuba dive with your guy? While you might have a little trouble actually finding someone to marry you underwater, you can say your vows on the beach and celebrate with a dive right after. Most all-inclusive island resorts provide scuba lessons, and since you've already paid for everything, you might as well take advantage of the opportunity. It's no reception; it's something you'll remember much more vividly.

In the air. Say your vows on a plane and take the plunge, preferably with a parachute attached. Or, take off for a hot-air balloon tour of the area.

Ⓔ **FACT**

Anything you can dream up you can turn into reality. You can have some fun and get really creative with your elopement. Plan a night for you and your fiancé to throw some ideas back and forth. You may be surprised to find just how imaginative he is.

Wedding Wear

So you're choosing a creative, kind of unusual spot for your elopement. What *are* you going to wear? A word of advice: If you're going the nontraditional route, you may find that the big, heavy wedding dress is not going to suit the occasion. Walking down the sandy beach dragging your train behind you is not only going to be more trouble than it's worth, it's also going to ruin the dress. If you're taking the time to plan a creative elopement, take some more time to think about what kind of clothing you're going to be most comfortable in. Remember—this day is about the two of you; you're not dressing up for anyone except your new husband.

Do I Have to Wear a Halter Top?

Just because you're choosing a wedding in Las Vegas—or another popular elopement destination—doesn't mean that you have to play the showgirl role in your wedding. Before you take off on your elopement getaway, do your research. If you're planning this elopement (as opposed to just hopping on a plane and seeing where the day takes you), you should have an idea of what's available in the area so that you can plan accordingly.

Traditional elopement hot spots like Las Vegas and Niagara Falls, for example, have a plethora of wedding services available. You can go to the wild extreme and wear your slinkiest outfit, or you can book a classy little chapel where you'll be comfortable wearing a nice dress. Look online or call the visitor's bureau in the area where you're planning your elopement. They'll be able to send you brochures with all of the appropriate information so that your wedding dress will match your wedding site.

Where Are My Hiking Boots?

Planning on saying your vows in the thick of the woods or on a mountaintop? You shouldn't dress much differently than you would for a normal day of hiking. If you're an inexperienced outdoors person or climber, take the time to get prepared. You are *not* going to make it up that mountain or through the woods in a pair of dressy sandals or heels. Likewise, you should leave the wedding dress at home. It's going to be impossible for you to climb even the smallest incline in such a heavy garment.

A good alternative—if you absolutely, positively have to have a dress—is to pack a light frock (preferably one that is wrinkle-resistant) in your bag, which you can change into when you reach your destination, season permitting, of course.

ALERT!

The outdoors is no place to skimp on absolute necessities. You shouldn't, for example, leave your water bottle or extra layers or first-aid kit in the car just so you can squeeze your pretty dress into your bag instead.

Another idea for a mountain-climbing expedition is to forego all traditional wedding wear, since you're eschewing tradition anyway, and buy yourselves some "Bride" and "Groom" caps to wear. Or make personalized shirts. (If you think that "I Mounted My New Groom Today" is too racy, you can stick with simple stuff, like your names and the date of your wedding.)

Safety First!

Getting married on your skis? Again, you should be focusing on the elements more than your wedding dress. It's downright dangerous to ski in a long dress. While you can eliminate the chill factor by donning your long johns underneath your gown, are you really going to be most comfortable that way—or are you going to feel slightly ridiculous?

If "I Gotta Be Me" is your motto and you're set on skiing down that mountain wearing a gown and veil, the more power to you. But if you're undecided on the whole thing, think about just wearing the veil or purchasing a white ski jacket for the occasion (not exactly cheap, but nowhere *near* the cost of a wedding dress).

While you can certainly do anything you feel is appropriate, be realistic, too. What if the dress gets caught in your bindings? What if your veil suddenly blinds you as you're schussing along? A cast—although it's white—is not exactly the look you want on your wedding day.

I Think I'll Just Wear My Thong

Even if you're getting married on a tropical beach, wearing your g-string bikini is not exactly appropriate wedding wear. True, there are no hard and fast rules about dressing for your elopement, but you are getting married. You should be somewhat clothed. If you just can't bear to part with the thong, throw on a sarong while you say your vows, at least.

For those of you who won't be wearing a swimsuit to your wedding, consider looking for something outside of the traditional wedding dress realm. While a sleeveless gown might be cool enough for a sunset ceremony, that taffeta *swish* is something you should only hear indoors—or perhaps on a stateside beach in the cooler months.

Don't Go Overboard

Transporting a wedding gown to an out-of-town destination is difficult and a little risky. If you've ever haggled with an airline over a lost suitcase, you know that it's sometimes impossible to know when—or if—your luggage will arrive. Imagine your distress if your wedding dress ends up in Duluth, while you're in St. John.

Another downside of packing your big dress is that it's going to get wrinkled. No airline in the world will guarantee that your dress will be laid flat on top of everyone else's luggage and will arrive in immaculate condition. You'll be faced with finding someone to make your dress pretty again once you arrive at your hotel, and although some destinations do offer these services, it may end up being an added hassle.

Instead, try finding a gauzy dress, or something that's very light and airy—some type of material you'd wear to the beach on any given day, especially if you're traveling to the tropics and getting married during the heat of the day. You don't want to pass out before you legally become his bride. Added bonus: Materials like these are easy to pack!

Forget the Wedding Accessories

And if you're going for the ultimate no-fuss beach wedding getup, lose the veil, too. It's one more thing to de-wrinkle upon your arrival, and you can easily add to the exotic feel of your wedding just by placing a flower in your hair.

Likewise, ditch the heels. You're never going to make it through the sand in them without looking like Jerry Lewis in his heyday. Your fiancé might start to wonder what he's gotten himself into—and the sweat you'll see on his brow will have nothing to do with the noonday sun.

Who's in on This?

Eloping, of course, doesn't necessarily mean that you've decided to keep everyone in the dark until you arrive home married. Still, in the event that you have decided to keep your elopement just between the two of you, you may want to consider letting just one or two carefully chosen people in on your plans.

 FACT

> You may want to avoid the unnecessary calls from home, but it's never a good idea to leave town without letting someone know where you're headed. By giving your itinerary to a tight-lipped friend or sibling, you'll be within reach for a true emergency, but blissfully out of touch for frivolous conversations.

An officemate—again, someone who doesn't revel in gossip or idle chitchat—is another person to consider trusting with your information. If something does pop up in your office, you'll have someone running interference for you. Only the most thick-headed boss would hunt you down on vacation for anything less than a true emergency, and your officemate can either offer to cover for you while you're gone, or, in a heroic effort to save you from nuisance calls, she can blurt it out: "Don't call her to ask about paper clips! She's eloping!"

Dealing with Snags and Delays

Alas, despite your best planning efforts, something keeps popping up that prevents the two of you from leaving town and becoming Mr. and Mrs. Wedded Bliss. Whether it's a tragic turn of events (a death in the family) or a work-related issue, you're stuck, and your wedding is on hold—precisely because no one knows your plans and no one will understand why you're taking off on a pleasure cruise when your company is in serious financial trouble. Is fate conspiring to keep you apart? Was eloping a mistake? Don't bet on it.

Hang On, You'll Get to That Altar

Debbie had been planning her elopement with Alex for about three months. They had been together for about four years, and finally decided that they wanted to get married—without the wait, without the hassle. They planned a trip to an all-inclusive couple's resort and counted the days until they left—the first time they planned on eloping.

Two days before they were to leave, Alex's uncle passed away. Debbie had never met the man, and Alex barely knew him, but his mother had lost her brother, and she was devastated. There was nothing to be done. "Here we had planned on coming back from our trip and announcing our marriage," Debbie recalls, "and we couldn't exactly come out with the news that we had to go away because we were getting married Sunday. We talked about it, actually, for about two minutes. We both knew that it was the wrong time to tell Alex's mom. So we had to cancel."

Ⓔ ALERT!

If you're ready for a spontaneous elopement, you probably aren't a slave to plans, so take it in stride if there's a need for a last-minute change of plans. If the airline lost your luggage, you may consider getting married in the clothes you're wearing, or visit the local stores for a new wedding outfit—or come up with an alternate solution.

The next time they planned on eloping, they decided to go to Las Vegas. "We figured we could just do it at the last minute, that we only really had to book a hotel room and our airline tickets. We felt like it was less planned and a little safer."

And what happened? "An ice storm hit our area the Friday we were supposed to leave. It lasted through most of Saturday, the airport was closed until Saturday night, and since we both had to be back to work on Monday, we had to cancel again."

And the third attempt? "The third time was the charm!" Debbie laughs. "But it was also the least planned attempt. We had to renew our marriage license by that time, because it had expired. We got the license . . . and we got married *literally* the minute we were legally able to."

Keep Your Wits

Whether you believe in fate or not, don't let your mind play tricks on you. If everything else is going well and a snowstorm prevents you from leaving town, chalk that up to Mother Nature. *Don't* throw away the love of your life because things didn't work out perfectly. Life is full of little problems.

It's when things don't *feel* right that you should start to ask some hard questions of your relationship. There's a fine line between being accusatory and being right, so tread carefully in this area. If your fiancé has been called in to perform emergency brain surgery, for example, don't assume that he's postponed the wedding because he doesn't really want to marry you. But if he *keeps* putting it off, nixing several sets of elopement plans, you need to address some larger issues in your relationship.

Chapter 6

Easy Escapes

As elopements grow in popularity, it's becoming easier to find all the necessary information for planning a quick wedding in almost any area. And if you're looking for more than just a drive-through wedding chapel and two anonymous witnesses—if an actual wedding with guests at an exciting locale is what you have in mind—you're also in luck. Destination weddings are becoming a huge trend, complete with professionals to take care of your every need.

Popular Destinations

Since so many couples are choosing destination weddings these days, the most popular elopement sites have extended their wedding services. It's easier than ever to plan a getaway wedding that includes a plan, a menu, and a guest list, so that your closest family and friends can stay with you at a resort where you'll get married. All you need is Internet access or a good travel agent.

Ⓔ ESSENTIAL

A growing trend at many wedding hot spots is live Internet hookup to nuptials in progress. This means you can call your mom and dad from your limo on the way to the wedding chapel and give them the chapel's Web address; they can log on and watch you say your vows live on their computer.

Las Vegas

You hear elopement? You think Vegas. No doubt about it, it's pretty darn easy to wake up and find yourself married in this town. In addition to being one of the states with no waiting period after you obtain your marriage license (and by the way, the Clark County clerk's office is open twenty-four hours on the weekends), there are countless wedding chapels to choose from, so you'll be sure to find one that suits your style. You can go the traditional route, with a dress and flowers, or you can wear your T-shirt and jeans. It's up to you, and the professionals in Las Vegas are there to make it happen. Consider the options for various Vegas weddings:

- You can have celebrity impersonators as your witnesses—or your minister.
- Many chapels offer traditional elegant weddings.
- There are indoor and outdoor locations.
- You can get married any time—day or night.
- Many sites have large reception facilities available if you plan on inviting friends and family.

The reason Las Vegas is so popular as a wedding destination is because it's so easy to get married there. If you're a bride who's dreading the thought of planning and executing the whole big production, you can have things completely taken care of for you in Vegas. Many wedding chapels offer packages ranging in price from a few hundred dollars to several thousand, and may include the following:

- Video and photographs of your wedding
- Reception for two (or 100) guests
- Tuxedo and wedding gown rentals
- Tour packages while you're in town
- Limousine service
- Wedding cake
- Champagne
- Flowers
- Music

Do some shopping around and find a package that includes what you want. Many chapels offer a weekday discount and a discount for military personnel.

Ⓔ FACT

Even if you go all out and choose one of the more expensive packages, you'll *still* be spending far less money than you would have on a traditional Big Wedding back home—plus you'll have the added excitement of eloping. You can't beat that winning combination.

The Caribbean

Many resorts in the Caribbean make their living from making couples happy. Accordingly, most are more than happy to go the extra mile to help you plan your elopement. Prices for these destinations vary wildly. If you're looking for a very private and exclusive island, for example, expect to pay a *minimum* of several thousand dollars. If you're looking for a simple ceremony at an all-inclusive resort, your nuptials may cost much less.

Some resorts have a wedding package that's included in the price of your stay, as long as you're planning on staying for the week. Talk about all-inclusive! Generally speaking, wedding packages in the Caribbean look very similar to Las Vegas packages—after all, most brides want similar services, so packages tend to include the basics (flowers, music, decorations, pictures).

One nice perk that many Caribbean resorts offer is a wedding coordinator to help you with your planning, which is included in the price of your wedding. This coordinator may help you obtain the officiant and documents you will need for your island ceremony, and the coordinator will also be on hand to help you with your basic necessities on the day of your wedding. Your dress is horribly wrinkled? The coordinator will find a steamer for you. Your hair is a mess from the humidity? The coordinator will know where you can have it fixed in a jiffy.

Most island weddings are geared for the smaller ceremony and will include a "reception" for fewer than ten people, including cake and champagne—though if you're planning on bringing along the entire family, most resorts will accommodate all of you. The resort you're staying in may also offer you and your new husband a wedding dinner and/or breakfast in bed the day after you say your vows.

If you have any lingering doubts about eloping, they will disappear as you're sitting in your hotel room eating mango with your new husband, or when you're gliding toward the swim-up bar in the pool with him.

European Getaways

Ah, to see Paris in the springtime, and return home married. Many couples opt for the romance and adventure of Europe—a continent rich with tradition and history. Think about reciting your own vows in a centuries-old church in England. Or maybe you'd rather say, "I do" in an Irish castle. Is Italy more your style?

Imagine the romantic gondola ride you'll take after the two of you marry in a palazzo overlooking the water.

There are companies that specialize in helping you plan a European elopement. Look online, or ask your travel agent. You can expect to find packages that look fairly similar to Las Vegas and Caribbean wedding packages—something for every price range and for every religious belief. In addition to the basics, European wedding packages may offer the following:

- Witnesses and an interpreter
- Elaborate multicourse wedding meal for the bride and groom
- Luxury cars to transport you to your wedding
- Assistance with necessary documents

Ⓔ ESSENTIAL

Since you've hopped the pond to elope, chances are you'll be staying for a little vacation. Honeymoon packages are also available and often include car rental and a private guide of the area for a day, along with accommodations in a classy hotel.

Let's Cruise, Baby!

Cruise lines often offer wedding coordination services. You can choose to marry on the ship (some of these floating cities have beautiful wedding chapels), or in one of the ports where the ship will dock. Wedding packages are often available, which, of course, can range from the bare necessities to an all-inclusive vacation. Call your travel agent or the cruise line of your choice for complete information.

Off the Beaten Path

But maybe you want to avoid the most obvious destinations and would like to find something a little different, but still a reasonable locale for elopement. In that case, check out some of these places. You may not be the only ones to have chosen one of these particular sites, but you won't be standing in line behind thirty other couples, either.

Destination: Canada

Niagara Falls has long been known as a popular honeymoon spot, so if you're planning on eloping, why not kill two birds with one stone? You'll find the Canadian side of Niagara Falls filled with tourist attractions, and the sight of the falls will astound you. Very romantic.

You may also want to check out the Canadian Rockies, where outdoor and extreme weddings are popular. Think about riding horseback to your wedding or careening down the rapids in a raft. Maybe you'd like to go four-wheeling before—or after—you say your vows, and then soak in a natural hot spring. In this rugged region of the country, almost anything goes. And if a wintry wedding is what you dream of, you won't find a more beautiful or appropriate setting.

 FACT

> If you're not into the chill of winter, you should avoid Canada until the springtime, when you'll be delighted to find an abundance of summer activities, such as golf, canoeing, and hiking.

Natural Wonders

Maybe you'd rather check out the Rockies on the American side of the border, and in the state that has become synonymous with the awe-inspiring mountain range. Colorado, like Canada, offers both winter and summer outdoor adventures.

And wouldn't it be interesting to be married at the bottom of a canyon, or in a beautiful vineyard? How about saying your vows in front of Old Faithful (appropriately named for the occasion at hand)? Many couples opt for an aesthetic setting for their elopement. National parks provide a fabulous—and somewhat unique—backdrop to your special day.

Consider the Details

You're planning on saying your vows in the Caribbean, or in Europe. Or maybe you're going clear across the United States. Wherever you're headed, it's quite a distance from your hometown. You want to invite some friends and family—but should you?

Are you going to foot the bill? You can very realistically rent a large home or a block of hotel rooms or a group or bungalows and treat your guests to a week (or weekend) of wedding fun. You'll most likely still end up paying less than you would have for a huge wedding, but it's not going to be an inexpensive affair by any means.

Destination Wedding Expenses

Which leads to the obvious question: Are you trying to save money by eloping, or are you trying to do something a little different? Obviously, if money is not an issue, you can invite whomever you'd like and not sweat the bill, but if you're eloping on a budget as most couples do, hosting a big crowd doesn't make good fiscal sense. If you're not in any kind of financial shape to be paying for a big lodging bill, don't do it.

Ⓔ ALERT!

Don't expect your friends to drop everything to attend your elopement in an expensive location. Even when couples choose a more traditional wedding route, travel expenses (including a stay at a local hotel, which is almost certainly less expensive than the island resort you're eyeing) often prevent guests from attending.

And if you're not planning on paying for your guests' stay, then you're on shaky ground. After all, if they had come to your Big Wedding, you wouldn't have expected them to pay for the food at the reception. A good rule of thumb is to expect to pay for any guests you invite to any wedding—whether it's down the street or across the globe. Whether or not you can afford it is your call.

If It's More Convenient

If, on the other hand, you're looking to invite your friends from every corner of the globe, they're looking at incurring travel expenses anyway. This is a situation where you can open up those lines of communication and ask your friends if it might be better for all of you to meet in a central location. It will be a lot easier for your friends who are living in Japan, Australia, and Idaho to attend a wedding you're planning in the Napa Valley, for example, than it will be for them to fly to your home in Alabama. (And for your friends in New York and Ohio, there's not *that* much difference in the travel time.)

Ⓔ ESSENTIAL

This is where you can offer to pick up part of the tab. Maybe you want to offer to pay for their meals or their hotel bill, but since you wouldn't be paying at all if they were traveling all the way to your home, it's an extremely nice gesture on your part.

There's a Place for You

The most important thing to remember when choosing your elopement destination is that it should feel right to you and your fiancé. Don't run with the crowd on this one—but don't back away from something you think you'll love simply because it's a popular spot. The most frequented areas are equipped with professionals who know exactly how to make your day feel unique.

The Power of Good Research

When you hear stories about particular destinations, consider your sources. If your very stuffy cousin came back from the Caribbean complaining about the music and the nightlife, are you getting a fair assessment of the area?

It's hard or almost impossible to narrow down the list of the most popular elopement/wedding destinations, because marrying elsewhere is such a growing trend, and it's a very personal decision. You may look at a list of elopement hot spots that is jam-packed with sunny locales, and think, "You know, I burn so easily . . ." Or you may find yourself reading about a "popular" spot in a region of the world where you'd never travel because of the cost, the additional hassle of coordinating overseas documents, or time restraints.

Make a Decision That Suits You

Deciding to elope to Timbuktu sounds intriguing—until you get on the plane and realize just how far it is, and how long it will take you to get there, and that there aren't espresso shops on every corner. If being taken completely out of your element isn't your thing (in other words, if unfamiliarity breeds contempt in you), don't expect the act of eloping to bring you around to your more adventurous side (which, truth be told, doesn't exist).

On the other hand, if you're a crowd hater, think twice before hopping a train to elope in the Big City, where you will be forced to bob and weave your way through throngs of other tourists, and you'll have to make a conscious effort to find quiet time for you and your new husband.

Ⓔ ALERT!

When choosing a destination, investigate on your own. It's all right to rely on the opinions of others—as long as you're not depending on someone who is the polar opposite of you to advise you in your travels.

Listen to your dominant personality traits. You don't want to spend your wedding trip miserable and out of sorts. Unless you're planning on buzzing in and out of whichever town you decide on, think of this as you would any other trip. Yes, you may be so excited and your head may be so far in the clouds that some things that normally bother you will fall by the wayside, but don't count on it. There's an equally good chance that you'll be putting extra pressure on yourself to have a good time because you're eloping—and if the town isn't the right fit for you, pressure will build quickly.

Take Control

If you're thinking about a quiet elopement, you may want to avoid the bright lights of Las Vegas, but in the event you're headed off to an elopement that isn't exactly what you pictured in your demure wedding fantasies, you don't have to buy into the whole sitcom-type wedding that you're trying to avoid. If you don't want a minister who's dressed as a showgirl, look for another chapel.

Likewise, if you don't like the idea of saying, "I do" on a cruise ship but you're definitely up for the cruise, look for an alternative. Perhaps you can find a quiet spot on one of the islands you'll be visiting and have your private wedding there.

The great thing about popular elopement destinations is that they offer plenty of choices. You don't have to spend a fortune to have a classy elopement; you will be able to find someone in your price range who will perform a simple, tasteful ceremony, if that's what you're looking for. Nor do you have to have a small wedding if you're looking to do something completely different and a little outrageous. It's like a wedding smorgasbord—take your pick.

Weekend Getaways

So far, this chapter has covered some popular elopement destinations—with the emphasis being on destination. Many couples are actually planning their destination weddings a year in advance. They're focusing on leaving town and having what will amount to a vacation and small reception with their family and close friends. But maybe your idea of elopement is different. Maybe you're just looking to leave town Friday and come home Monday married.

Ⓔ QUESTION?

What if our elopement is a last-minute thing and we haven't had time to do much research?

You can still find what you're looking for fairly easily. Stop by the local visitor's bureau and ask for some assistance. Remember: Couples like you are the bread and butter of these towns. Help is there for the asking.

No Need to Wait

If you're looking for a no-hassle, no-waiting, no-frills elopement, you'll be able to pull something together. There are twenty-six states in the United States that do not require you to sit tight for several days after you apply for and receive the marriage license. (For more information, visit ✍ *www.usmarriagelaws.com.*) Any one of these states could be your potential elopement locale.

Get Moving

Once you've decided to elope and picked the destination, just go for it. Call the county clerk's office and get the information you'll need to apply for a marriage license. Here's what you'll need to ask:

- What kind of identification will we need?
- Will we need to bring one or two witnesses?
- Do both of us need to be present to apply for the license, or can one person get things rolling?
- How much does the marriage license cost?
- What are the office hours?
- How can we get in touch with a justice of the peace or another officiant?

 **ALERT!**

> If you're eloping to a town with a waiting period, make sure that the waiting period includes weekend days. Otherwise, you may come home Monday just as single as you were on Friday.

Every state has its own procedures. Often different counties within the same state will have their own standards of operation, so don't depend on the information you get from friends or acquaintances. Verify the facts yourself. This is one process you don't want to have to repeat over and over again.

Where Are We?

Your elopement is what you make of it. Even if you find yourself in a region not known for its beautiful scenery and romanticism, you can still find something special about it. Let's say you've chosen to get married in a teeny little nondescript chapel in the Smoky Mountains. You're in the midst of nature's beauty—take advantage of it. Are you eloping somewhere in Ohio, and wondering if you should have hopped the flight to the Bahamas? Nonsense! Find a cozy little restaurant and enjoy your wedding dinner together.

The fact of the matter is, every area has something to offer. Some couples prefer to elope somewhere without crowds, without attention, without high prices—these are the reasons they chose to elope in the first place. That way, they can concentrate on each other, in which case all you really need is someplace to lay your heads for the evening.

May and her husband did elope in the Smoky Mountains. She says, "It started out as a cross-country trip, and by the time we hit the middle of the country, we were just itching to get married—anywhere we could. It just felt like the right moment to us. I knew that if we waited and planned for a year, it wouldn't feel the same.

"We were in Gatlinburg, Tennessee, and it seemed so perfect for a little impromptu wedding. We decided to hang out there for a couple of days. We did the paperwork, we found this little wedding chapel, and we got married. Then we continued on our trip, which was even better at that point because we were newlyweds. It was just quick and kind of crazy, but it was so right for us."

Simple Civil Ceremonies

So you're short on time—not only do you not have time to take a weekend road trip, you barely have time for a lunch break. And yet, you want to get married as soon as is humanly possible. City hall is the place for you. Maybe not what you dreamed of, but you can certainly make your civil ceremony romantic.

Ⓔ ESSENTIAL

Many men have no idea what a wedding means to the woman in their lives, and since you've both opted to have a small ceremony, he may assume that you aren't expecting any traditional accoutrements. Communication will prevent any tiffs on your wedding day.

Don't Skimp

Even if you've chosen to get married by a judge in the town court, take the time to prepare for the moment. You probably won't opt for the big gown and veil, but you may still want to primp a bit—fix your hair, do your makeup, buy a new dress, find a boutonniere. If you want to carry flowers, go ahead and get them, or make it clear to your guy that you'll be expecting some.

Schedule Late

If you can schedule your vows for later in the afternoon, there's a chance you'll both feel better about taking the rest of the day for yourselves, especially if you're choosing a civil ceremony because of crazy work schedules. Take the time to appreciate the significance of the day. Go for a walk or treat yourselves to a four-star hotel for the night. If you're inviting some friends or family to the ceremony, make reservations (in a restaurant that fits your budget) so that everyone can celebrate your good fortune with you.

Take Pictures

When couples elope to a destination that routinely hosts newlyweds, it's easy to find a photographer or a photo studio on a minute's notice, and many times the photos are included in the wedding package. When you elope locally and quickly, you may think that you'll have to do without those priceless pictures. You won't.

You may be extremely lucky to find a photographer on short notice who happens to have some time available for you. If you don't, grab your own camera. If you're inviting friends to the ceremony, ask them to take pictures for you. If you're not, don't feel bad about grabbing passersby and asking them to snap shots of the two of you as you make your rounds about town after the ceremony—and don't be shy about telling them your story. You'll find that more often than not, folks will be more than happy to take a picture of the newlyweds. Be nice and say, "please" and "thank you."

The Morning After

If you've chosen to elope in town because of time restraints, you probably won't have time for a honeymoon right away, but don't let that stop you from acting like newlyweds. Do everything in your power to make time for each other in the days and weeks immediately following your vows. You've made a huge commitment, and, hopefully, you're only going to do this once. Get into the newlywed groove—go out of your way for each other, cancel that meeting and have dinner with your new husband, hold hands in the grocery store.

Some of your behavior might be impulsive (like shrugging off extra work for a while), but this time will pass much too quickly, so don't lose your chance. The newlywed phase of marriage flies right by—and when it changes into a more comfortable but less exciting state, you'll miss it. If you don't take the time to steep yourself in this season of wedded bliss, you'll always wish you had.

Chapter 7

Elopement Fundamentals

Regardless of where you take the plunge, there are a few issues you'll need to tackle before you head out of town. This chapter goes over the checklist of what you absolutely, positively must take care of before you elope, like making sure you have a marriage license that will make your marriage legal. It also includes a few tips on buying engagement and wedding rings, finding someone to preside over the vows, and planning your honeymoon.

Marriage License

The marriage license is the document that will prove that the two of you are legally married. Oh sure, there's always the debate over what that piece of paper *really* means—does it really bring you closer, does it truly mean you'll be together forever, and so on? But, romantic idealism aside, you do need that paper if you're going to be legally married, which is the whole point of eloping. The following is an overview of general considerations when applying for a marriage license, so you'll still need to do your research very carefully. Laws vary from state to state and often from county to county:

License fees. Every state charges a fee for a marriage license. The amount varies from state to state, but runs under $100. Beware: Most states require that you pay for the license in cash and some will also accept a money order, so don't plan on whipping out your plastic to cover this expense. Without cash, you may be left high, dry, and still single at the end of the day (or week, if you're getting hitched in a state with a waiting period).

Identification. You will need, at a minimum, a valid photo ID. Some states also require your social security number and/or your birth certificate; some states only require the birth certificate if you're under thirty. Since this requirement varies in each state, it's essential that you check out the details and bring the right IDs.

Waiting period. Most states have one; some states don't. There's no way to figure this one out by guessing, so check it out before you pack your bags. If you're in a rush, the good news is that twenty-four states do not have any waiting period, so odds are, you're within a day's drive of one of them.

Blood test. Once part and parcel of applying for the marriage license, the blood test and/or physical exam is no longer required in most states.

Ⓔ **ALERT!**

> Your failure to disclose a venereal disease or any physical condition that affects both you and your spouse (such as infertility) may render your marriage invalid when the truth comes out. It's best to be honest, even though you're not required to have a blood test for the purposes of obtaining the marriage license.

Other Requirements

Did you think you were done thinking about the marriage license once you learned that you don't need a blood test? Wait! There's more to know! These are smaller details, but every bit as important to your obtaining your license to live happily ever after.

Applying for the License

Some states require that both of you be present when applying for the marriage license. In other states, one of you can get the ball rolling (if you're marrying in the state your fiancé lives in, for example) by providing the pertinent information; when the other party arrives, he or she can bring the necessary paperwork for verification. If you plan on eloping to Nevada, you can actually apply for the marriage license online from the comfort of your own home or office—just make sure your boss is out to lunch.

Residency Requirements

Most places do not require couples getting married there to be residents of that state or county, but this isn't something you should leave to chance. If the two of you find yourselves driving through Wisconsin when you make the decision to get married right then and there, you'll be disappointed to learn that one of you needs to have thirty days' residency in the county where you intend to tie the knot.

 FACT

> Some states require you to have a witness present when you apply for the license. If you're planning on eloping in complete secrecy, you may want to choose a state that doesn't require you to bring anyone else along for the ride.

Previous Marriages

If this is your second time around, be prepared to show proof of divorce, death of spouse, or annulment when you apply for a marriage license. This isn't necessary in every state; Nevada, for example, only requires that you know when and where you were divorced—which should be easy enough for you to make a note of before you take off for your elopement.

Age Requirements

In most states, you need to be at least eighteen years old to apply for a marriage license; in Mississippi, the minimum age is twenty-one. Generally speaking, if you're under the minimum age requirement, you'll need a parent or guardian present when you apply for the marriage license.

Marriage Overseas

The discussion thus far has been geared toward couples who are thinking of eloping stateside. But what if you want to leave it all behind and elope to Europe, or Asia, or the Caribbean? There is good news and bad news, depending on your destination.

The good news: Eloping to the Caribbean is fairly hassle-free. The fees are a little pricier on some islands than they are in the United States. For example, a marriage license will cost you around $200 in the Cayman Islands. Also be aware that some islands have waiting periods and/or residency requirements—St. Barts requires that one of you be in residence for thirty days prior to your wedding. Several islands also require physical tests—Puerto Rico requires a blood test taken within the ten days prior to your marriage.

The bad news: Eloping to France? You're going to have to plan a long prewedding honeymoon. French law requires a forty-day residency (for both of you) in order to tie the knot on their soil. It's even more difficult to get married in China, unless one of you is a citizen. Foreign couples are generally not allowed to marry each other in that country.

Ⓔ ESSENTIAL

Since the Caribbean Islands are themselves making an industry of quick and easy marriages, couples' resorts on the islands go out of their way to ensure that your elopement is quick and easy. Many have wedding packages complete with a wedding coordinator to aid you in your elopement plans.

If you're planning to elope abroad, your best bet is to check with the American embassy in the country where you're planning to be married. They'll have information on the local marriage laws and customs, which will be incredibly helpful in your planning.

Finding the Officiant

You've chosen to elope because you want your wedding to be about the two of you, and not about the wedding hoopla. Once you've chosen a destination and worked out the legal details, you have to start thinking about *who* is going to preside over your vows. Whether you're looking for a very close family member or friend to stand watch over the nuptials or just anybody vested with the appropriate powers to pronounce you man and wife, you need to start looking. Now.

Sure, You Can Be a Minister

A decade ago, who would have thought that anyone could become an ordained minister from the comfort of his or her computer chair? Your friend Jimmy wants to be the one who marries you and your fiancé? Great. It doesn't matter if he's religious; it doesn't matter if he believes in anything. If he has the time (and by "time," we're talking about ten minutes tops), his online ordination is just waiting for him to find it.

He'll have to give his name and pertinent information, of course, but there's really very little else to it. Some sites require that the interested party send in a hard copy of an application along with a minimal fee (around $5); some sites will send an e-mail confirmation of the newly ordained status. In many states, this is all someone needs in order to perform a marriage ceremony.

Whether this is a good idea for your elopement is up to you. As always, it's best to check your local laws before you allow an Internet-ordained minister to pronounce you man and wife. You do want the marriage to be legal, after all.

Let's Go with a Professional

Looking to have a "real" minister or priest preside over your vows? Better check with him or her good and early. Their weekends are often booked with church activities, including other weddings.

In the event that you're looking to get married on the fly, you might have a difficult time snagging a priest. Many Catholic parishes have a minimal waiting period of six months, and most also require that the couple attend premarital classes.

Ⓔ ALERT!

Be aware that some states have laws stating that a minister must be associated with an actual church and an actual congregation in order to perform religious ceremonies. If you plan on being married in one of these states, an Internet-ordained minister is not your best option.

It never hurts to ask, of course, but when you're mixing tradition with eloping, you might run into a few roadblocks, precisely because so many other couples are going the traditional route and have booked their weddings far in advance; your minister simply might not have the time. Fortunately, you have other options.

Justice of the Peace

If you're planning on marrying in a wedding-friendly area like the Caribbean, rest easy. The island resorts have wedding coordinators who will help find an officiant for your wedding. This is often part of the wedding packages offered by these elopement havens. Check with your travel agent or with the resort itself. Likewise, if you're eloping to Las Vegas, you're going to find more officiants than you ever thought possible, all of them ready to preside over your vows.

If you're eloping locally or to a place that isn't exactly making a name for itself as an elopement hot spot, it's best to ask the county clerk when you apply for the marriage license. They will have the name of a justice of the peace and can help put you in touch with him or her. The rest is up to you.

Alex and Marty eloped in New England several years ago, and Alex, at least, found that it was easier than she had expected. "Marty was in the Navy and he went and got the marriage license, going early in the week before I flew in for the weekend," she recalls. "I got there, showed the clerk my ID and birth certificate, and signed on the dotted line. Marty had gotten the name of a justice of the peace when he started filling out the paperwork earlier in the week, and he made the arrangements with her. My plane landed at noon, and by three o'clock, we were married."

Who Needs an Officiant Anyway?

Of course, if you're off to elopement-friendly Colorado, you don't need anyone to listen to your vows. The two of you can pronounce yourselves married (after obtaining the marriage license, of course). Can you think of anything more romantic?

Don't Forget the Rings

Just because you've chosen to say your vows in a simple manner doesn't mean that you've chosen to live your entire life that way. You may still want a gorgeous wedding ring, and what's more, you may be better able to afford one since you're scaling back on most other wedding frills. Assuming you're going to have some say in the matter (many brides do these days), this section touches on what to look for in a ring and a jeweler—and some signs that you should keep on looking.

Ⓔ ESSENTIAL

If your groom feels that he can't afford to buy the big honking ring right now, let him give you what he's comfortable with. Don't measure his love by what he's willing and able to spend on your wedding ring—which, in stark contrast to his feelings for you, may be very limited.

Choose the Right Venue

Don't be fooled by the stores in the malls. Yes, they're convenient, and yes, they advertise the most, but they're likely to have the largest markups on their jewelry because they have the most overhead (they're paying very high rents and numerous employees) and the least amount of flexibility in their pricing. The employees in these shops are accountable to a corporation; they're also usually working on commission.

Conversely, the owner of a smaller store may be able to offer you a much better deal. He sets his own prices, often at a much lower profit margin than the big stores. And if you're serious about buying a certain piece of jewelry, he may be willing to work out a deal.

Ask some older folks for the name of a good jeweler. Chances are, they'll be more aware of who's been around for years and years, who's trustworthy, and they may also know of any problems that a jeweler has had over the years.

Know What You Want

Buying jewelry is not like buying a sweater. You're going to spend a lot of money on something that you hope is going to be around for a long, long time. Before you set foot in a jewelry store, take the time to research the particular metal and/or stones you're after. Imagine walking into a car dealership and saying, "Gee, I need a new car and I don't know anything about cars—and I want you to take a look and tell me what you think I need and what I should pay for it."

An honest dealer is going to help you make your first purchase. A less-than-honest dealer is going to look at you and see his or her new vacation home. Be on guard by having some inkling of what you're looking for and—more importantly—what you're willing to pay for it. It's up to you to have some ballpark figure of what a fair price is. How will you know this? Start as early as possible and shop around. And it'll also help if you know the jargon.

Ⓔ ALERT!

There are very honest and scrupulous sales-people out there who are in the business to sell quality jewels and metals; and then there are the guys who are going to tell you that the poorest quality items are in incredibly high demand—and will sell them to you at an incredible markup.

Karats and More

Karats are measures used to identify the purity of gold. A higher number indicates a higher percentage of gold in the jewelry, so a 14K gold ring is not as pure as the 24K one. If you are looking at diamonds, you will also need to consider the cut, color, clarity, and karats. The cut is the shape, of course. Color is often graded on a letter scale. Clarity determines just that— how clear the diamond is. And karats measure the gemstone's weight. Most jewelers will walk you through these criteria, but you want to walk into the store knowing a little bit about them.

Be aware that as you approach and exceed the one-karat mark, the price of the diamond increases exponentially. Yes, it's true—diamonds are forever, but there are also a lot of other places to put your money. Remember: Eloping is all about saving money; you don't have carte blanche to spend all the money you've saved by not hiring a marching band on a trinket for yourself.

 FACT

An honest jeweler won't try the hard sell with you. Instead, she'll assume you're going to shop around. If you run into a jeweler who encourages you to take a look around at other shops, listen to her carefully. She's probably the most trustworthy of the bunch and knows that the other places aren't going to be as forthcoming with you.

Faux Stones

You've seen the fake jewels on those television shopping channels. You've squirmed in your seat as you thought to yourself, "Who would buy this stuff?"

You'd be surprised. These phony gemstones sell like hotcakes—and if you're looking to save yourself (and your fiancé) a few thousand bucks, you might want to take a look at them. Many jewelers are starting to stock "laboratory created" gemstones because of the great demand for jewels that look pretty but are also affordable.

Karyn's husband, Dennis, bought her a faux sapphire and diamond bracelet when they eloped five years ago. "I would have killed him if he had spent the money on the real thing," she says. "We were looking at houses, and it would have been dumb to put off buying a home just so I could drape myself in real sapphires. But you know what? It looks real, and I love this bracelet because Dennis gave it to me. I'll get my real diamond one day. I'm in no rush."

Another reason to consider faux jewelry is if you have a slight problem keeping track of things. Alicia is one of these women. She says: "I lose *everything*. Even when I'm very careful about putting something somewhere, it goes missing. I'm not really into jewelry anyway, but I did want a diamond wedding ring—except that I was very uncomfortable about having to worry about where that ring was all the time."

She and her fiancé had a little talk and decided they would both be much more at ease if Alicia was not taxed with keeping an eye on a wandering diamond. Has the compromise paid off? Alicia laughs. "It has. I haven't *actually* lost the ring, but I have misplaced it a few times. And I *was* sick about it, because it's my wedding ring. But I wasn't thinking about what the ring is worth, and if someone was going to find it and sell it, and that kind of thing. I was just thinking, *I have to find my wedding ring.*"

Honeymoon Plans

The great thing about eloping is that you can make it a long vacation, which requires a lot of planning and finagling of your schedule, or you can do it on very short notice, which may mean that the honeymoon will be put off for a while. The important thing about the honeymoon is that you take it—it doesn't matter how little money you can spend on the trip; it doesn't matter if you have just a few days to get away. What matters is taking the time to recognize the huge step you've taken together.

Solid Planning

Your best bet, if you have the time, is to talk to a travel agent about your vacation plans. He or she will know about deals and the best time to travel to certain areas. You want to go to the Caribbean in August? Your travel agent will let you know if the resort you've chosen has a hurricane clause in its reservation policies.

If you don't know a good travel agent or don't have the time to track one down, there's another option available to you. Many travelers have good luck finding deals online. Some deals require traveling on short notice, so if you're flexible, you just might be able to take the trip of your dreams for very little cash.

Honeymooning on the Sly

You're not telling anyone about your elopement, and yet you're getting married in town. How are the two of you going to grab some snuggle time before you make your grand announcement?

Easy. Check yourselves into the nicest hotel or inn you can find. Order room service and relax. Revel in your moment. If you're not taking vacation time from work, for example, opting to honeymoon somewhere other than your apartment will make you sit up and take notice of this special time together. Instead of returning home to the same old pad on your wedding night, treat yourselves to something a little different. You don't have to spend the week there—just enough time to enjoy each other, free from the humdrum obligations of home.

There's No Time—at All

In the event that you have absolutely no time to honeymoon right after the vows (if, for example, you're in the middle of a project at work that your entire career is dependent on), plan something as soon as possible. Even if it's a few months down the road, even if it's not a globetrotting excursion, even if it's nothing more than a weekend in the next town over—plan it.

ESSENTIAL

A honeymoon is more than a luxury. It's a bonding time for the two of you. Once you find yourself knee-deep in life's little annoyances, it's going to be harder to recapture that truly amazing, romantic feeling that you'll have right after your wedding.

You're only going to be newlyweds for a short time. Don't put off the honeymoon indefinitely just because you didn't plan a huge wedding. Seize the day—before you find yourself more interested in wallpaper samples and mortgage rates than in taking a vacation with your husband.

True, lots of couples take late honeymoons and second and third honeymoons—but you're only going to be *just married* once. It's a special time; make some acknowledgment of it.

Getting Ready

It helps if you can plan for your honeymoon. If you know you're leaving on your weeklong vacation on June 1, try not to take on six new projects at work that all need to be completed the day before—or worse, two days after you come back. Guess what you'll be worried about while your spouse is dreamily watching the sunset and contemplating the rest of your life together? If you are expecting a busy period at work, plan your honeymoon at a slower time.

Remind yourselves that you're getting to know each other and your respective vacationing habits. If you've never been on a trip together, you could be in for a shock when you realize your new husband likes to get up at six in the morning to be the first one in line at the breakfast buffet. (Funny, he doesn't do that at home. And you're not about to queue up for bagels and coffee before the sun shows its first rays.)

Give each other room to breathe. Although you're on your honeymoon and it's very romantic and you're supposed to spend every single minute looking into each other's eyes, both of you need to realize that not everyone can tolerate being attached to someone else at the hip—honeymoon or not. You're not hormonal teenagers; even though one of you may feel that way, the other might just need thirty minutes alone every now and then. Clear communication on this issue will help the snuggly spouse avoid complete devastation and the feeling that he or she has been rejected by the not-so-snuggly-all-the-time partner.

(E) ALERT!

No matter where or when you end up going on your honeymoon, remind yourselves that you're off for a little rest and relaxation—and then figure out what that means.

Most importantly, don't expect your honeymoon to be perfect. You're newly married, and that's a huge life change. Go into your honeymoon expecting to have a little fun and a little romance, but don't put too much emphasis on either one. Let the vacation take care of itself; you can't plan the most romantic moments. Just let them happen.

Chapter 8

Personalizing Your Elopement

Even though you're nixing the conventional wedding by eloping, you may not want to eliminate all tradition. There are many ways to personalize even the simplest and quickest of elopements. Write your own wedding vows and read them to each other during the ceremony. Invite a few close friends to join you at the elopement ceremony. Grab a disposable camera to record the event. You don't need wedding professionals to personalize your wedding. All you need are your imagination, a little romance, and each other.

Wedding Vows

Many couples opt to have the standardized wedding vows, which require a simple "I do" or "I will" from the bride and groom—and little else. If you fear you'll have a hard time just remembering to breathe at the altar, you may feel this is your best option. If, on the other hand, you're looking to really make this day unique, there are other, more personal options available to you.

Write Your Own Vows

You're eloping because you just despise the fakery of the traditional wedding. You didn't want to sit in a banquet hall surrounded by mobs of strangers and long-lost relatives; you wanted this day to be about you and your new husband. So don't be afraid to take the time to express your feelings about him and your hopes and dreams for the future.

Ⓔ ALERT!

If you've decided to write your own vows, start early. While some women are adept enough to sit down ten minutes before the ceremony and put their feelings into words, many aren't. Start thinking about what you want to say at least a week prior to the ceremony—if you're not eloping on a moment's notice, that is.

You may be eager to get going on this little project because you have so much to say. Or you may shudder at the thought of writing something romantic. If the latter is true, here are some tips on writing your own vows:

- **Use your own voice.** Don't use fifteenth-century idioms or an excessive amount of romantic-sounding (but thoroughly confusing) foreign terms unless you're both familiar with this type of language. Your fiancé won't know if you're channeling Shakespeare or trying to tell him something.

- **Limit yourself—a little.** Give yourself a three- to five-minute time frame. Yes, this is a big, big day, and this is possibly the most important thing you've ever said to your fiancé—which is exactly why you should keep it short and sweet. There will be time enough after the ceremony for your thirty-minute presentation on all the things you love about him.

- **Read it out loud first.** The funny thing about the written word is that it doesn't always translate smoothly into speech. If you can wrangle a friend into listening to a rough draft of your vows, do it. She may be able to pick out something that doesn't sound quite right—and it may be something that is easily reworded.

- **Give yourself a break.** If you're just not a born writer, don't sweat it. You don't need to be a poet to compose your own vows. Write down your feelings, some memories, and your vision of the future. He'll love it simply because you made the effort.

Including Your Favorite Verses

Some couples are highly literate. Their idea of a good time is sitting under a shady tree and reading verses of poetry to each other. If you and your fiancé have a particular poem that you're wild about, go ahead and include it in your vows. Still, even if you choose to use poetry as the foundation for your vows, you may also want to add your own words before and after any verses you include.

Ⓔ ESSENTIAL

If you're a religious person and in search of some inspiration for your verses, look no further than your Bible. For instance, 1 Corinthians, chapter 13, contains a great passage on love that's often used for weddings; the Song of Songs is also filled with love poetry.

Completely Tongue-Tied?

If you find yourself completely unable to commit to reciting your own vows—because you're shy or you're completely drawing a blank—but you want to personalize your exchange of promises, it's all right to find an appropriate poem to recite instead. Look for poetry books at the library or online, or ask a friend who's into sonnets or ballads to help you out.

Don't think of using a poet's words as taking the easy way out. You're still highly involved in the process, and you're making an effort to find the exact words that express your feelings—even if they're not your own.

Sticking with Tradition

You're thinking, "Hey—we don't want a traditional wedding! That's why we're eloping!" Fair enough. But eloping doesn't mean that you have to throw every custom out the window; it simply means that you aren't listening to what the big bridal magazines are telling you to do. Eloping isn't about eliminating options for you and your fiancé. It's actually about choosing the options you want and doing away with those you don't.

Dressing Up

Some couples choose to elope in jeans or shorts; some wear swimwear on the beach; others hop over to city hall in their business suits. If you're thinking you'd rather follow the traditional dress code and show up in a dress, that's within your range of options as well.

Because many women elope to avoid paying outrageous sums of money for a big tulle dress, you may want to explore some other avenues when choosing a frock. Try an upscale dress shop or department store. They may have just the thing you're looking for—something that's well made, the perfect shade of white (or ivory), a little lacy, very sophisticated, and well under $1,000.

If you're looking for something really unique, try a vintage clothing store. If it's good enough for Hollywood stars (many of whom opt for vintage dresses when the big award shows roll around), it's good enough for your wedding day. As you shop, think unique instead of traditional. Focusing on finding a wedding dress may prevent you from seeing the dress of your dreams right in front of you.

 FACT

> There's no law stating that you must wear white on your elopement day. If you see a pink, orange, or yellow garment that grabs you, go for it. You're already bucking tradition by eloping. Find something that suits your taste as well as the setting you've chosen.

Speaking of vintage, what about asking your grandmother if you can borrow her frill-less wedding dress, the one you've always dreamed of wearing? She'd probably be more than happy to loan it to you—that is, if you plan on letting her in on your elopement.

Bridal Stores Are an Option

You may also want to take a look in some bridal stores, but don't limit yourself to the wedding dresses. Sure, there may be a very informal wedding dress (or a very formal one) that jumps out and screams, "I'm it!" But you may be better off looking at the other racks in the shop.

Mary found her dress in the pages of a bridal magazine. When she showed the magazine to the saleswoman at the bridal shop, the woman was confused. "You do realize that this is a bridesmaid dress, don't you?" Mary recalls her saying. "She couldn't believe that

I wanted to buy this dress for my wedding. But it looked perfect to me—it was a cream color, it had a lace bodice and a silk skirt, and little beads around the neckline. I bought it off the rack, I had a few tiny alterations done, and we eloped the following week. It was that easy."

Flowers for the Bride

You don't have to walk down the aisle empty-handed. If you're eloping quickly, pop into any floral shop and grab a bouquet for yourself. You like the look of a single flower? Even better. If you're looking for something very elaborate, you'll need more than a day's notice; call your florist as soon as possible to inquire about your special order.

Ⓔ ESSENTIAL

If you're having an outdoor elopement in the springtime or summer, go with nature and pick your own bridal bouquet, local laws permitting—you don't need to end up with a citation for violating the wildflower laws on your wedding day.

Dancing and Romancing

You're eloping in your hometown, you're not inviting any guests, you have to go to work the next morning, and you feel as though your wedding day is lacking the excitement of a whirlwind trip. Take charge. Find yourselves a nice, quiet restaurant for an intimate little dinner and some dancing. Or book a suite in a four-star hotel for the night and enjoy the room service. Make your wedding night a special and incredibly romantic one, even if you are only too well aware that reality will be creeping in with the morning light.

Including a Few VIPs

Traditionally, eloping implied that the families of the bride and groom were left in the dark about the ceremony until it was too late for anyone to object to the marriage. Today, things have changed. If you're eloping for financial reasons or because you just don't want to hang around and be engaged forever, consider inviting a few familiar faces to the wedding.

Your Dad, Your Escort

If you're eloping and inviting the family along, there's no reason not to include them in the wedding itself. Even though you didn't want your dad to invite his business partners to your wedding, you may still want him to walk you down the aisle. The aisle doesn't have to be long or formal, just as long as he gets to give you away at the end of it.

Bridal Party

Since you're looking to pare things down by eloping, you're probably also looking to eliminate the parade of bridesmaids. However, you can feel free to ask one or two of your very closest friends to serve as bridesmaids or witnesses. Since they're not hosting a shower for you, and since they won't be wearing tangerine taffeta, you can call them whatever you want.

Ⓔ QUESTION?

What about including groomsmen?
Your fiancé can also extend this offer to one or two of his friends. They'll be touched that you wanted to include them in your small affair.

A Teeny, Tiny Reception

You can absolutely invite your closest friends and family to share in your celebration. Invite them to join you for your wedding dinner in a restaurant of your choosing. It doesn't have to be the most expensive place in town, but you might want to put the kibosh on any fast-food restaurants. Dinner should be your treat, of course—just remember how much you're saving by not hosting an *additional* 200 guests over at the country club.

Feel free to call ahead and ask the restaurant if they have any special packages available for your party. Some facilities may be able to provide you with a small wedding cake, for example, if they also have a catering service.

If the restaurant can't hook you up with a cake and you just need to have one, inquire about bringing your own. Some places will allow this, others won't, and some will charge you an extra fee.

Wedding Mementos

You've chosen not to publish an engagement picture in all of the local newspapers. Maybe it's because you and your fiancé are hardly having an engagement period and are skipping right to the happily ever after part, or perhaps it's because you cringe at the thought of making such a huge deal out of something that should be so intimate. You're not planning on paying big bucks for a photographer to follow you around every moment of your wedding/elopement day. So how are you going to remember every special thing that happens?

Is That an Album or a Giant Coaster?

Most brides will tell you that while they wouldn't sell their wedding album at a yard sale, they hardly ever look at it. Some brides may choose to leave the album on display in their home, set obtrusively on the coffee table, but many will eventually put it away in their closet, and maybe pull it out on their anniversary every year.

Cameron and Penny spent what they considered to be "a small fortune" for their wedding photographer and album when they were married. Cameron says, "I think we lost track of what we were spending, quite honestly. This guy was expensive—and I have to say, he was good. He took pictures all day, of us, of the guests, of everything and everybody. The really funny thing is because *we* didn't know a lot of the guests, we ended up with a lot of very expensive 'crowd shots' of complete strangers.

"My mom really loves the album, and Penny's mom does, too. Penny and I like the pictures of us together. She was actually having a hard time with two of her bridesmaids, so that's what she remembers when she looks at the pictures of herself with them. We have one wedding picture in a frame on our mantel—that's it. Do I think we got our money's worth from this album? No."

 FACT

> You don't need to document every second of the day—unless you want to, of course. Some brides find that having a professional photographer follow them around all day is highly disconcerting at best, and irritating at worst.

And there you have it. Wedding pictures don't have to be expensive or even formal to be treasured. Penny chimes in on this point: "My favorite pictures of our wedding day, actually, are the ones that other people took. And it had nothing to do with the photographer; he was great, and his pictures are beautiful. It's just that in the other pictures, Cam and I both look more relaxed and natural, because we weren't posing for most of them."

There's a lesson here for the frugal bride and the bride who's eloping tomorrow. If you're eloping on short notice, you probably won't be able to book a photographer no matter how hard you try. Don't feel too badly about it. Have a friend take some pictures.

Elopement on Film

Video cameras are pervasive in this age of technology. Everyone has one, and for those of you who don't, there's good news: They're relatively inexpensive. Instead of hiring a videographer, buy your own camera. Say you're planning on eloping locally. The two of you can easily make a wedding day tape of where you're going, where you've been, and what you're up to in between.

In the event that you're getting a video as part of a wedding package, it's a good move—according to many brides. When Jenny eloped six years ago, she and her husband Rob opted for a wedding package that included several posed shots of them and a video of their ceremony. She says, "You know, still pictures just don't tell the whole story. We have watched that tape so many times, and I *still* get goose bumps—Rob's voice is all shaky in it, because he was so nervous, and I cried while I said my vows. It just captured the moment so much better than the pictures did. I would recommend a tape to anyone who's considering one, even if it means they'd have to skimp on the photo package."

Wedding Souvenirs

But what if you've eloped so quickly that you didn't bring a camera, and there's not a camcorder in a 100-

mile radius? Will you have to rely on your already-fal-tering memory to remind you of where you were married and your wedding day activities? Partially.

You need to use your imagination and get a little crafty. Imagine if you were getting married in an age without cameras of any sort. How would you recall this day?

 **ALERT!**

> You will have to declare your purchases when you leave the country or island you're visiting, and there are limits as to what you can bring back with you. Check with customs in the country or on the island you're visiting.

If you're getting married in a big city, pick out a trinket or two—and make it something a little more extravagant than a key chain. Snow globes are always a good choice; they elicit a romantic feeling. As you look down on the miniature city inside with the flakes swirling all around its tallest spires and its smallest houses, you'll almost be able to see the little bride and groom coming out of the wedding chapel. Or how about a porcelain vase with the name of your wedding locale embossed on it? Or a hand-painted plate depicting the rose garden where the two of you said your vows?

Jewelry is often a nice choice. Cara eloped to the Virgin Islands, where gold is considerably cheaper than it is stateside. "I'm into chains. I don't wear earrings, and I can't stand to have a ring on," she says. "Jon and I went and picked out a beautiful gold chain in one of the jewelry shops, and I wear it almost every day."

But why stop there? If you've eloped with very little prior notice or intention, you'll be needing things for your new place. If you're off to Ireland, for example, you'll want to stock up on linens. Off to France? You'll be needing some crystal. You can often have your goodies shipped directly to your home, so you won't need to worry about how you're going to fit all your loot into your suitcase.

Creative Keepsakes

Creativity is the key to a special remembrance of your big day. Don't feel silly about making a little collection of memorabilia—anything from a button that falls off your husband's sleeve during the cab ride to letters you write to one another right before or after the ceremony. Use your imagination and let yourself be romantic.

Keep a Journal

One interesting way to keep your thoughts and feelings alive for yourself and for generations to come is to keep a written journal of your elopement trip. How were you feeling, exactly, when the two of you initially hit the road? Were you excited, scared, overwhelmed? In addition to describing your feelings, you may want to include the following information:

- Details of the ceremony (time, those present, flowers, music, etc.)
- Your impression of your groom's state of mind
- An account of how you spent the rest of the day
- A day-to-day update on your status as newlyweds
- Other thoughts—were you scared to go home or excited to share the news?

Sometimes a written account of events captures the smallest details—things you never would remember otherwise, like the look on your fiancé's face when you walked into the wedding chapel, or the funny waiter at the restaurant where you celebrated the wedding. It's these little, seemingly inconsequential details that will make you smile years down the road, long after you realize that that look on your husband's face was due to his sunburn and not to any wedding-related anxiety.

Mother Nature

Whether you've said your vows in a garden or you took a walk through a field after your ceremony, a flower will make a romantic little keepsake. It doesn't have to be a fragrant rose—it can be a dandelion that you press in a book and save forever. The meaning comes from the occasion, not from the flower itself.

If you've said your vows on the beach, take enough home with you to fill a small jar and set on your bookshelf or nightstand. Not only will it remind you of the happiest day of your life, it'll be a real pick-me-up in the dead of winter.

What Else?

The fact of the matter is that anything can be a souvenir of your special day or trip; it's more about your state of mind than the actual item. Many women routinely save things that remind them of a special time—ticket stubs, subway tokens, dinner receipts, bottle caps, matchbooks, you name it.

Pick and choose things from your trip that strike you as being a little romantic and that will be easy to store away for the future. This means nothing perishable. It's not a good idea to save the remainders of the hot pretzel the two of you shared on your walk through the park. The mice will have a little party in your closet once you store it away.

Ⓔ QUESTION?

Want to have a fun time all around town?
Hire a limo to drive you and your new husband—and some friends, if you choose—to all the hot spots in town, where you can celebrate your marriage in style.

Special Sites

Anyone can elope to a high-traffic wedding chapel, and the reason many couples choose to do so, of course, is because it's quick and it's easy. Most chapels will allow you either the option to personalize your ceremony, or to hurry things along in the event that you just want to say, "Yes! I take him for better or worse!" While you're in control to some degree, there's another way to really personalize your elopement: Choose a spot that means something to you.

Where Did You Meet?

Are you both dog lovers who met in the park while walking with your canine friends? Or are you a couple of bookworms who met at the library while reaching for the one available copy of Proust's complete works, volume 12? Were the two of you thrown into a blind date on the terrace of a little restaurant on the waterfront? Did you meet while you were working at the hospital and he came staggering through the emergency room doors with a splinter in his thumb?

Love at first sight is a rare and overwhelming emotion. Many couples confess to *growing* in love, instead of being hit by Cupid's arrow the first time they met. If the place of your first meeting means so much to you that you return there frequently just to look at the spot where you were standing when you first saw him, because you can't believe there isn't a burn from a lightning bolt, why not consider saying your vows there?

If you met in the park, have your officiant or minister meet you there. Your favorite restaurant may be willing to work out a time—before the dinner rush or after the place closes—for you to say your vows on that charming little terrace. You met while you were both working in the hospital? Look into eloping in its chapel. And what about the library? While you may not be able to schedule an elopement among the stacks (especially if it's a university library and you're planning on eloping during finals' week), you may very well be able to say your vows under the lovely magnolia tree out back.

Ⓔ **ESSENTIAL**

> The key here is to get a little creative and to be a little flexible. You will have to respect and adhere to the rules of the various institutions and/or businesses, which means you're going to have to ask about what's allowed and what's not.

Be prepared for the possibility that you won't be able to get what you want. There may be insurance liability issues or legal issues that the owner of an establishment isn't willing to take on. In this case, it helps to have a Plan B.

Plan B

In the event that you are not able to get married in the place where you met or where you first realized that you were madly in love (if, for example, you met in a grocery store and you just don't feel right about saying, "I do" next to all that produce), keep thinking. You've undoubtedly had some incredible experiences together outside of your first meeting place. Have you discovered a love of hiking together? Do you cherish those Sunday afternoons on his boat? Was your first kiss on the pitcher's mound of your high school baseball field many, many years ago?

Maybe you'd like to climb a mountain together and say your vows at the top. Or maybe you're interested in taking your vows on the dock before setting off on a sunset cruise. Or maybe you're thinking of asking the minister to meet you on the ball field (after clearing it with the proper authorities, of course).

 FACT

> If you're choosing a very unusual spot—like the grocery store—you're going to hear from the peanut gallery. Ignore negative comments, if you can. If you can't, have a stock comment at the ready—something along the lines of, "It was the freshest wedding ever!" Chances are, you wouldn't be choosing a creative place if you weren't a brave romantic at heart.

Is It Right for You?

When you choose to say your vows in an unusual or unassuming place that means everything to the two of you, you're going to get a lot of feedback. Some of your friends and acquaintances will sigh, "How romantic!" Others will offer you raised eyebrows, snickers, and rude comments like, "A baseball diamond? How *original*!"

Here's where you're going to need a tough skin. You're choosing to elope to a spot that's appropriate for the two of you, for your own reasons. You don't need anyone's approval to make it happen.

If you're unsure of having an exceptionally unique elopement, listen to your inner voice. Go with your best judgment. You should be 100 percent comfortable about the entire ceremony. If you feel as though it's turning into some sort of stunt—for shock value or for comical effect—make other arrangements.

Chapter 9

Coming Home Married

Assuming you haven't eloped with your entire family in tow, your elopement may come as a complete surprise to them. Even if you've been dating your now-husband for years, it's still possible that your friends and family honestly never saw this wedding coming. So how are you going to tell them you've made your relationship permanent? It's time to think about the best way of preparing those you love with the news that they may not be ready to hear.

We Have Something to Tell You

You know your family. You know how they react to certain situations, and you know how to phrase things just the right way so that their response is tempered a bit. Remember the time you ended up in jail for protesting and you needed your dad to bail you out? You were able to talk your way out of that. That wasn't so bad, right? So what's so hard about telling them you got married?

Ⓔ ESSENTIAL

This is a pretty big deal—in fact, as far as deals go, they don't get much bigger. You eloped and you didn't tell your family. Weddings make people emotionally unstable and completely unpredictable. Expect this. Prepare for this. Get a coat of armor if you have to, and get ready to deal with the fallout.

When to Break the News

This totally depends on your family's dynamic. Maybe your parents *love* your boyfriend and have been after you to marry him for several years. In this case (and possibly only in this case), they may be pleased to receive a phone call from you after you've taken your vows in the Chapel of Love.

If, on the other hand, they've been trying to set you up with the nice guy who works at the pharmacy, or that guy at the health food store, or the one who lives down the street from them—in other words, they want to see you with anyone other than *your* guy—you can bet that they're not going to be thrilled to hear that your beau dragged you off to elope. (And this is exactly how they will interpret your wedding story.)

While you don't want to interrupt your elopement trip with any negativity from back home—and since you're the only ones who know anything about it, you're in complete control, for now—bear in mind that the longer you wait, the harder it will be. If you've been back from Vegas for two weeks and you *still* haven't told your family and friends that you're married, you're going to have to eventually explain your delay in relaying that pertinent information.

 FACT

> By delaying the news longer and longer, you are hiding the fact that you're married. While you may have justifiable reasons, you also need to be adult enough to step up to the family podium and announce your marriage. You promised to stick with your man through all kinds of trouble in life—there's no time like the present to stand by him.

Think of it this way: You wouldn't have married this man if you weren't in love with him. Being in love with him means that you're proud to be his wife. The longer you wait to tell your family about your marriage, the *less* they're going to think of him—partially because *you* obviously didn't think enough of him to present him as a member of the family when he became one, or very soon afterward.

How to Break the News

If you suspect your parents won't be thrilled with your elopement, don't call them from your limo just before or right after you walk down the aisle. Even though you may feel a little guilty about not telling them just yet, you should enjoy your time with your new husband.

When you arrive home—back in reality—you should have some sort of plan for telling your parents that you've acquired a husband over the weekend (or however long you've been away). If you think things are going to go badly no matter what, keep it simple. Arrange to have a quiet talk with them at their home or at yours. If you think things will go better with your husband at your side, have him there; if you think he'll only inflame the issue, go alone.

Ⓔ ALERT!

If you fear a horrible confrontation, better to keep your parents and your husband separated until the shock wears off, so that the initial conversation doesn't result in a heated argument full of accusations—and a lifetime of hard feelings.

This is not cowardice on your part or his, by the way—you wouldn't light a match next to a powder keg, would you? If you know your parents are going to be furious about your union, nothing your new husband does will be acceptable to them. If he sits quietly, they'll think he's a wimp, and if he gets into a confrontation with them, they'll think he's a violent predator.

How Not to Tell Them

Generally speaking, you should avoid the following methods of announcing your elopement to your parents:

E-mail. This is a great way to keep in touch, but incredibly impersonal for this particular purpose.

The grapevine. Calling your sister from the wedding chapel and asking her not to tell your mom and dad that you've eloped will almost guarantee that she *will* tell them.

Casually mentioning it. If you think you can slip your news in while you and your mom are shoe shopping, think again. It's big news—treat it as such.

Mom? I'm at the Altar

If you're expecting a negative reaction from your families and you know there's no way around it, you may as well enjoy your elopement trip before you break the news to the folks back home. Chances are, if you've eloped under these circumstances, your excited phone call will be met with dead silence, or worse, a crying fit, on the other end.

You're going to have to deal with reality soon enough. Give yourselves a few days as a happy and relatively carefree pair of newlyweds before you encounter the Wrath of Mom.

Informing Your Estranged Family

Even if you haven't been in touch with your family for years, you should still tell them about your elopement yourself. Don't let them hear it on the street, and don't send your mother a written announcement. That's heartless, regardless of how you really feel about some of your immediate relations. You're one up on them, anyway: You obviously know the big news. If you think they're going to react negatively—or if you think they might shrug their shoulders and ask, "Who cares if you got married?"—you can prepare yourself in advance.

Your Long-Lost Mother

You may have nothing to say to her; you may not have seen her for years. You may harbor ill will against the very genes that link the two of you. But she's still your mother. Call her and tell her you're married. No matter what's happened between the two of you over the years, the manner in which you announce your marriage to your mother reflects on you. Take the high road and give her a call when you return home or visit her in person to tell her your news.

ⒺESSENTIAL

> If you haven't really spoken to your mother in the last five years, think twice before you call her from your hotel suite on your wedding night. There's no telling what her reaction will be, and this isn't a time to play Russian roulette with your own emotions. Call her when you get home.

Out-of-Touch Siblings

You should also take the time to inform your brothers and sisters of your nuptials. Yes, everyone knows that you and your sister were never able to see eye-to-eye on anything, and if the two of you never spoke again, it would be too soon. However, omitting her from the family loop on this issue is a slap in the face—and something she will throw in your face until one of you kicks the bucket. No matter that the two of you aren't really speaking; she'll be sure to mention it at every family event, and you can be sure that anyone who will listen will hear how completely devastated she was to learn about your marriage from a formal announcement.

If you're mature enough to be a wife, you're certainly mature enough to give your sister a call and tell her you're married. And you're also mature enough not to be goaded into an argument with her when she makes her sarcastic remarks. Just say, "Goodbye, Sis," and hang up.

Your New In-Laws

It's up to your husband to take the initiative on announcing your marital status to his family, but you don't have to hide in the corner until he does. You can be right there by his side when he calls his mother, but he should be the one to speak with her first. Mothers are unpredictable creatures, especially when it comes to weddings, and even more so when it comes to their darling boys. If she thinks even for a nanosecond that you somehow trapped her son into marrying you, all bets are off. She may change from a sweet, lovable nurturer into a lioness—and guess who'll be her prey?

Ⓔ ALERT!

Don't doubt your husband's methods of dealing with his parents. Sons often know how to handle their moms in exactly the right way, and if he sounds happy, chances are she'll eventually be happy for him—and for you.

If you've entered into this union knowing that his family wasn't hip to the idea of you two becoming man and wife, steel yourself for an icy reception, and remember the old adage, "Kill them with kindness."

Smoothing Things Over

You've broken the news, and things went as badly as you thought they would. Your mom cried, your dad didn't say anything, and your husband's parents started yelling at him in a foreign language that he refused to translate for you. Where do you go from here? Who should make the next move?

His Family

You knew his parents didn't love you to pieces, but you weren't expecting this kind of reaction—tears and screaming and the cold shoulder. You're a nice person, after all. Shouldn't they just be happy that their son has found the love of his life?

Although you are understandably hurt and angry at this point, try to stay calm. You've married this wonderful man, but you have to remember that he was theirs for many, many years prior to your elopement. It's going to take them time to adjust to the idea, so give it to them.

If you're looking for long-term peace, keep your head in this emotionally charged time. Don't give his family any ammunition to dislike you. This means you shouldn't call his mother just to fight with her—even when you're hopping mad.

Yes, she is completely in the wrong by sending him pictures of his old, and still very single, girlfriend. Take the time to realize that this is also your mother-in-law's way of baiting you. If she reels you into a fight, guess who's going to look like the instigator? That would be you. Keep your distance until her sanity returns.

Don't blame your husband for how his family treats you. He's probably just as upset about it as you are, and if you take it out on him, you're attacking your only ally who shares your new surname—if you took his name, that is.

Your Family

How are you going to convince your parents to accept your new husband when they won't even look at him, and they have told you in no uncertain terms that they don't want to know his name? You've always relied on your parents to be the foundation of your life. When they go off the deep end and take their support from you, it's completely devastating. And in the meantime, you have a new spouse that you love so much. Why can't they see how great he is?

 FACT

> The best thing you can do is to give parents time. Don't expect them to show up at your apartment later in the day with an armload of wedding presents. Give them time to be angry, and time to sort out their feelings.

To answer this question, you have to look at it from your parents' point of view. All they know is that you've eloped. Remember, elopement means different things to different people. This is all they're processing in their minds right now. They don't have a favorable opinion of your method of marriage. Your husband is just a blip on their radar right now. They're hurt and they're angry. Maybe they're talking to you about this; maybe they're not.

When they are ready to talk, let them. Let them get everything off their chests. Don't scream back and don't interrupt. Listen to what they have to say, and be an adult. The best way to keep them thinking that you're a frivolous kid is to act like one. The situation is volatile enough; if you're looking to settle things down, take a deep breath and count to ten before you speak.

Support Each Other

If, in the end, your family has decided amongst themselves that your husband is to blame for everything, you need to stand beside your man. He'll never be able to earn their respect if the two of you don't present a united front.

If it's his family that's making you miserable, don't automatically lump him in with his gene pool. When you're dealing with in-laws who see you as a she-devil, you're bound to be emotional and angry. You married their son, but that doesn't mean that you'll be able to win them over.

If they're truly difficult people, your husband knows it. You don't need to constantly call it to his attention or accuse him of taking their side simply because he's ignoring them instead of constantly bickering with them. He's made his choice, and he chose you—that's why his family is upset, after all.

Your Friends, His Friends

Remember way back when, before boys came into the picture? You and your girlfriends were devoted to each other. Many women still share a level of loyalty when they move into adulthood, and it's this sense of female allegiance that is at risk when your best friend finds out you were keeping a big secret (your elopement) from her.

It's even worse when you have a group of close friends who are suddenly questioning your honesty. Many will understand why you didn't announce that you were actually eloping when you left on your vacation; others are going to be hurt that you didn't trust them with the secret. Your husband's friends are less likely to be hurt by the news; their reaction may be closer to complete shock.

Ⓔ ESSENTIAL

The only thing the two of you truly have control over is your relationship—and a loving, stable marriage goes a long way in proving to everyone else that you made the right choice.

In any event, realize that your primary obligation is to each other. If the two of you decided to keep mum about the elopement, you both need to respect that decision, and your friends need to come to terms with that. End of story. You don't need to offer any further explanation. Let them be angry for a day or two. When they ask (and they will), feel free to share the details of your wedding.

Getting over Wedding Fantasies

It can't be said enough: Weddings can make people a little crazy. Maybe one of the reasons you chose to elope was to save your own sanity—or to avoid your mother's (or your future mother-in-law's) insanity. You may think that because you've tied the knot in the simplest way, these issues are behind you. They may not be. Even if your mom supports your decision all the way, she probably would have liked to see you get married. How can you deal with your parents' emotional state?

Explain Yourself

Your mom has had visions of you prancing down a 300-foot aisle since you started dating this man you've just eloped with. She had your dress picked out, she knew what flavor the cake was going to be, and she was in the process of interviewing band leaders when you walked in her door . . . married. You've crushed her dreams, and she's taking it hard.

Tell her why you eloped. List all of the reasons. What your mom is looking for are some good reasons why you would do this to her—why you wouldn't want a huge wedding. She keeps telling you that she didn't have a Big Wedding because her parents couldn't afford it. Here she was, willing to pay for everything, and you went and eloped.

The key here is open, calm communication. Let her keep talking. Eventually it's going to occur to her that she was planning the wedding she wanted. Let her lay it all out on the line, and then you can respond by telling her why you chose to elope.

ⒺALERT!

This is not the time to accuse your mother of being overbearing and controlling. Avoid this line of argumentation at all costs, or the only thing you'll accomplish is producing more hard feelings. Show off your adult side, even if she is acting a little childish.

Don't expect miracles. What you're doing is laying the groundwork for your mother's breakthrough down the line. Mothers who claim to be devastated by the elopement itself (it's not the man you married that she has issues with) are dealing with their own fantasies, and they can only resolve these by themselves.

What you're trying to do is give her some food for thought—so that the next time she sits down to cry over the wedding you should have had, she might also think about the wedding you did have and how ecstatic you are with your new husband. Although she won't admit it, these thoughts will start to creep into the back of her mind, because this is what moms really want for their daughters. If she knows you're truly happy, her wedding issues will fade with time.

Tell the Story

Don't be stingy with the details. If your parents weren't there when you took this man for your husband, tell them everything (or at least everything appropriate for their delicate ears). Consider covering these points:

- How he proposed, or how you proposed to him
- Why you decided to elope
- How you decided on your unusual elopement site
- What you were wearing
- What the officiant was like
- Any special details, like personalized vows you wrote for the marriage ceremony

If you have pictures, whip them out. If you have a tape of the wedding, even better. Show them the dress you wore while you took your vows. Did you bring them souvenirs? They'll appreciate them later.

Ⓔ FACT

Including them in your elopement—even after the fact—will allow your parents to see that it really was romantic, that you really are happy, and that you didn't do this just to spite them..

Taking Your Show on the Road

Don't forget that you have to do the same for his family. Mothers of the bride are traditionally the women who lose their heads over weddings, but don't doubt for one moment that a mother isn't just as possessive of her son. One sure way to ease yourself into his family is to discuss your elopement with them—when they're ready. A few tips:

- **Act excited.** Even though you're nervous, don't clam up now. These people want to know that you love their boy as much as they do.
- **Put on a tough shell.** Remember, they're still accepting your elopement. Don't take any negative comments too personally.
- **Do unto others . . .** If you took the time to show your parents the video of the vows, show it to his parents, too. This is the kind of thing that will come up when your mothers eventually get together, and it is the very thing to get you in his family's good graces.

One Big Happy Family

You've broken the news, you've lived through the initial stages of both families' reactions, and now you're moving on to other issues. How on earth are you going to combine his family and yours when his family blames you for the elopement, and your family blames him? Are you destined to live your life running interference, hoping that your husband doesn't answer the phone when your mom calls? Or worse, what if your mother actually meets his mother? Can these two worlds be melded into one—without incident?

Don't Rush Things

One thing you have to remember is that you're going to be married to this man for the rest of your life. You have time to work out the family issues. Although the only thing you've done is to marry the man of your dreams, you have to realize that some people have been hurt or shocked by your elopement. Don't expect too much in the first few weeks or even months. Take this time to work on your marriage, and let your parents and your in-laws take the time to get used to the idea of your elopement.

When everyone's emotions have settled down, extend a dinner invitation to your in-laws. Have your parents over on another night. Let each family get used to the idea of your new home and your marriage before you think about having both families over to meet each other.

When you do decide to have everyone to your home, go with your instincts. If you think a small gathering will be incredibly painful for everyone involved (if you can't see his dad and your dad making small talk for hours on end, for example), make it a larger get-together. Having a few extra faces around will take the pressure off of the initial meeting, and no one will feel forced into conversation. Invite some comfortable old friends or your siblings—anyone who can ease the night along.

This is a good way to hide the fact that your sets of parents have absolutely nothing in common. If they can make charming chitchat for ten minutes and then move on to other conversations with different people, no one (including you) will end the night feeling worn out from desperately trying to keep the discourse from dying.

Give Them a Time Limit

If his family is having difficulty accepting you as their daughter-in-law, give them the space they need without cutting them off completely. Continue to offer invitations for dinner; send them a holiday card; don't tell your husband that he can't see them until they love you, too. Above all, don't take their reactions too personally, at least in the first few months. Unfortunately, you're simply an easy target.

Learn a lesson from Dawn, who eloped with her then-boyfriend, Garry, several years ago. Their reception as a married couple from Garry's mother was chilly, to say the least. Dawn apparently was not what Garry's mother had hoped for in a daughter-in-law. Dawn says she is the "wrong everything—wrong religion, wrong ethnicity, wrong political affiliation—you name it, I'm on the wrong side, according to his mom." Dawn tried to make peace with this woman. She dutifully attended weekend outings with his family; she sent birthday cards; she kept a smile on her face. For a while.

"You know, it got to the point where I realized that the harder I tried to make her like me, the less she thought of me. So I stopped going out of my way. I told Garry that his mother was his responsibility, and that I wouldn't be buying her Christmas gift—he would have to do that himself. I also told him that I wasn't going to go to her house for dinner all the time anymore just so she could ignore me.

"I didn't make him choose between us; I just made it clear that if she was going to be rude to me, I wasn't going to continue to put myself in situations where she could do that."

Ⓔ ESSENTIAL

> If you've offered them every kindness and they still treat you badly, it's truly their loss—remember that. Scale back your efforts after six months or so, but don't stop them altogether until it's very clear that they intend to continue ignoring you forever. You don't have to beat your head into a wall.

The result? Garry's mother was irate at first. Who did this girl think she was, not showing up to dinner? But other family members spoke up in Dawn's defense. "The family knew she was acting badly," Dawn says, "and I didn't have any problems with anyone else; it was only Garry's mom. I think no one knew what to do, until I put an end to it myself, and then it was like I had a cheering section. Eventually, she started treating me like a human being. We get along well enough now."

If it's your family who's treating your husband unfairly well after their initial shock should have worn off, you have the ability to step in and have a word with them. Yes, you love them, and yes, you want everyone to get along, but your obligation is to your husband. Let your family know that. You may be surprised at their response when they realize you mean business—and when they realize you intend to stay married to this man.

Keep Your Perspective

It's easy to stand back and look at someone else's family turmoil and think, "Well, cut ties with these people. It's that simple." It's another thing when you're in the middle of it. If you're extremely close to your parents and they're suddenly pretending you don't exist, it can be an absolute nightmare.

Ask yourself this: What have you done, really? You haven't killed anyone; you haven't been convicted of a felony; you haven't brought shame to the family, no matter what anyone else says. You eloped. A big deal, yes, but not something that should elicit wails of sorrow from anyone for months on end.

Ⓔ ALERT!

Shocking your family with an elopement doesn't qualify as a "heinous" act. Keep reminding yourself that as you try dealing with those members of your family who just can't take a surprise.

Soon-to-Be Grandparents

If the stork is knocking on your door, you're understandably in a hurry to get the family issues behind you and focus on the future. This is not the time to stress over his mother's ambiguous comments or your father's refusal to acknowledge your marriage—and everyone knows it. Those who are willing to upset you during this time don't deserve a response.

Once the baby makes his or her appearance (or even beforehand), those grandparents just might be beating a path to your door, suddenly willing to put the elopement issue to rest. And if the comments that have been hurled in your direction—or toward your husband—have not been incredibly insulting, you just might let them in. If that's what it takes, don't question it. Be happy that your child has grandparents who are wise enough to realize when it's time to let bygones be bygones.

Family Problems Solved

Try not to worry so much about what happens early on in your marriage, and try to be the better person when you need to be. Years from now, you won't be able to believe there was a time when your in-laws wouldn't come for dinner.

When you're able to chat with your mother-in-law about the wallpaper you've chosen for your family room, or when your mother asks if you're hosting Easter dinner at your house, you can be reasonably sure that the tide is starting to turn.

You'll know you're making headway when his mom decides to have you over for dinner (presumably to show you how it's done) or when your dad asks your husband to go fishing (presumably to have a little chat with him). It may not be an easy transition for anyone, but if your respective families are important to the two of you, make the effort—for each other.

Chapter 10

Making Post-Elopement Rounds

You're home, you're married, you're happy. How are you going to let the world know it—and how is the world going to let you know they're happy for you? You might consider sending out wedding announcements, and keep it at that. But what if your mother is just dying to host a post-wedding reception for you and her husband? If you can grin and bear it, let her. It will probably help her deal with the disappointment of missing out on your wedding.

Wedding Announcements

You wouldn't want your Aunt Patsy to hear about your marriage down at the corner tavern, would you? Doesn't your husband's great-grandmother deserve to know that she's acquired a great-granddaughter-in-law? Wedding announcements are a nice way to divulge your marriage to some of the people you *would* have invited to a Big Wedding.

The Purpose

The purpose of sending wedding announcements is to let people know that you're married. This is not a request for a gift, and you shouldn't expect checks to start flowing in the week after you mail out your cards.

Ⓔ FACT

Think of these announcements as a life update. For example, you send cards to people with your new address when you move so that they know where to find you. You don't expect your friends and relatives to send you new lamps and throw rugs; you're simply saying, "This is where I am." Your wedding announcement lets them know that someone else is there with you now.

Who Should Receive an Announcement?

Try this as your criterion for sending an announcement: Would you feel funny if this person heard you were married from someone other than you, or do you imagine this person opening your announcement and asking himself or herself, "Who *are* these people?"

Ⓔ **ESSENTIAL**

> You don't necessarily have to mail an announcement to everyone who would have made it onto a Big Wedding guest list. Your mother may have wanted to invite your third cousins whom you have never laid eyes on, but that doesn't mean that you need to alert them to your marital status.

Since you've eschewed the Big Wedding and its trappings up until this point, keep your wedding announcement list on the simple side. Friends and family (but only family members that you actually *know*) should receive announcements. Business associates, acquaintances, and neighbors do not need to be on the roster. They'll most likely feel as though they're being hit up for a wedding gift.

Have your new husband draw up his own list of recipients. If he has no clue as to who should get an announcement and who shouldn't, you can certainly guide him, but let him do the actual brainstorming.

How Do I Say This?

Again, keep it simple. There's no need to use the wedding announcements on the society page as your guide. You will not need to include the type of fabric you were wearing when you said your vows, nor will you need to mention what your parents do for a living and/or where they reside. The following sample announcement includes just the basics: Joan J. Jones and John Q. Public were married in a sunset ceremony on the island of Barbados, April 20, 2001.

These are the relevant facts, and you should stick to them. Anything more (like mentioning the four-star resort you stayed at or including your home address on the announcement) may come off looking tacky and/or like a request for cash.

If this seems far too simple for your taste, there are ways to jazz things up a little:

- Include a romantic verse or lyric.
- Include a wallet-sized wedding photo.
- Choose colorful or unusual stationery.

Ⓔ QUESTION?

Where do I find wedding announcements?
You can have wedding announcements printed at any shop that prints invitations. You can also find announcements online.

Feeling Artistic?

So you and your new husband are quite artsy and you want to make the announcements yourselves to give them a truly personal touch. Is that all right? Are you within the bounds of post-wedding etiquette?

Sure, as long as you aren't planning on making your announcements from pipe cleaners and construction paper. As happy and lighthearted as you're feeling right now, you might feel as though you could write your announcement on notebook paper—it would still capture everything you're feeling. True enough.

ⓔ ALERT!

If you choose to make your own announcements, keep it on the semiformal (respectable) side. You can't blame the print shop for your ill-conceived use of crayon.

Remember though, the folks on your mailing list aren't living in a newlywed haze. Mailing out an announcement that looks like the artistic brainchild of a third-grader is going to send several unintended messages: You're silly, you're taking the institution of marriage lightly, and you have really bad taste.

If you're looking to make your own announcements because you think it will be cheaper than having them printed, you may be wrong. Call around and get some prices from print shops in your area. If you can find a discount printer, you may find that the cost of making those announcements is about the same as having them done professionally.

A Post-Wedding Reception

You eloped to avoid a reception, and yet the moment you walked through the door with your new husband in tow, your mother was off and running with plans for your family to meet and greet your spouse—at a reception. Should you dig in your heels and refuse to be a part of this? Isn't what you want the most important thing? If you're answering in the affirmative, think again.

Making Mom Happy

First things first. Some mothers react so negatively to their child's elopement that they won't speak to their son or daughter—never mind the new spouse in the picture. If your mom is looking to host a reception for you, she's obviously acknowledging your presence and not behaving as though there's been a death in the family. Give her credit for that much.

Whatever her reasons are—whether she wants to host this reception because she never had one, or because she wants the rest of the family to meet your husband, or because she's simply excited—don't say, "no" to her until you've taken a day or two to think about it.

Yes, you're tired of her line: "It's not every day my child comes home married. When you have a daughter of your own, you'll understand." But she's probably right. Give her a break, if you can find it anywhere in your heart to do so.

It's Important to Communicate

It's understandable that your mother wants to fete you and your new husband, but if the two of you eloped because you didn't want to be the center of attention, are you destined to an afternoon of wedding bell hell?

Not necessarily. Now that you've come home with a husband, you may be caught up in a postnuptial maelstrom. You're planning on sending wedding announcements, your mother is planning a huge party, you're working on getting your husband's name on your lease, and on top of everything else, you're way behind at work. Welcome back!

Ⓔ ESSENTIAL

No matter how nicely (or how badly) your mother is behaving, there's no doubt that she would have loved to be at your wedding. It was your choice to do things the way you wanted; no one's arguing that. But maybe—just maybe—you could bring yourself to attend the party she wants to give you.

In a time like this, it's so easy to overlook the fact that you can easily stop trouble in its tracks. Instead of just listening to your mom ramble on about the huge reception she wants to have for you while you also sort through the mounds of vacation laundry in your bedroom and then move on to that pile of work sitting on the coffee table—in other words, you're not really listening to her at all—take the time to give her some gently worded feedback.

If you're not comfortable being the center of attention, tell her. It's possible that she'll acknowledge everything you're saying and will scale back her party plans to suit your preferences. It's also possible that she'll tell you how silly you're being—but it never hurts to voice your opinion in a diplomatic manner.

You are attending this reception because your mom wants to have it for you, but you don't have to be her puppet on a string. Speak up if something on her agenda really bothers you, or else you may find yourself complaining at the worst time—during the reception itself.

Who's Paying?

If your parents or in-laws want to host a post-elopement reception for you, you shouldn't expect to pay for it. Weddings are a different story, of course; many couples pay for the entire thing out of their own pockets. However, those couples have the added benefit of choosing the site, the band, the food, the day, and so on. This is essentially a party you chose not to have by eloping, and in fact, it may be part of something you wanted to avoid altogether.

There's no reason you can't chip in on the cost of a delayed reception if you want to. For example, if you are actively planning this shindig along with your parents and you want to have a live band instead of a sound system, whip out your checkbook. But if your mom is essentially planning a family party with you and your spouse as the guests of honor, she shouldn't expect you to foot the bill. This is something you are well within your rights to refuse.

What to Wear

If this event is to be a casual reception, wear something that's dressy enough, but not too dressy. In other words, if you and your husband are the guests of honor at a luncheon-type reception, you should not be wearing a wedding dress with a train, and he shouldn't be wearing a tuxedo. A suit might work well for you, and your husband will look great in dress pants and a jacket. You may have a dress that you just love and that fits the occasion perfectly.

 FACT

> If the reception is being held in a formal place like a country club, you should step up your apparel a bit. Your husband might want to wear his best suit, for example, and you might want to buy a more formal dress for the occasion.

The bottom line is that you should take the time to look your best. It may not be your wedding day, but your marriage is the reason for this party. Even if you're attending under (silent) protest, acknowledge the fact that the guests are coming to see you and wish you well. Don't show up in jeans and a ripped T-shirt.

I Do, Redux

Oh, some mothers are bound and determined to see you walk down the aisle, even though you've technically and legally done it already. If your mom is planning a little renewal of your two-week-old vows to go along with the reception, try not to sweat it too much. Remind yourself how much this means to her—and also remind yourself that you really did get to have your wedding the way you wanted it when you eloped.

Man and Wife, After All

Did you elope because the two of you and your mother—or his mother—couldn't agree on an officiant? Were you and your husband looking forward to having a friend of yours preside over the vows, while your mother wouldn't hear of it? Or were you absolutely determined to be married in a church that your mother disapproves of, to put it mildly?

Seeing as you've already been legally wed at this point, it's possible that your mother may drop the issue of the vows altogether—but if someone is insisting on a renewal of vows, this may be the perfect opportunity to have the ceremony you wanted in the first place. Having your eccentric minister buddy (or the priest from your church), the thought of whom gives your mom a migraine, preside over your vows at this point may seem like a formality—which it is—and thus not anything worth fighting over. Just remember: It's not worth fighting over at this point; if your mother is still having palpitations at the thought of this particular officiant, let it go.

Look on the Bright Side

You may be completely against the whole idea of a reception and/or a repetition of your vows for the masses. After all, if you had wanted it done that way, you would have had the Big Wedding with the dress and the bridesmaids and the reception—right? On the other hand, maybe doing things a little out of order is the best way to have the best of both worlds.

Show Up and Enjoy Yourself

One nice thing about attending a reception in your honor after your elopement is that a lot of the pressure is off. You and your husband have already had your wedding day, after all, and you've most likely had some time to snuggle up and enjoy being newlyweds.

You might really enjoy a reception at this point in time, because you won't feel as though this is the most special day in your entire life. That means you won't feel as though everything has to go perfectly or you'll burst into tears. You aren't likely to be an emotional wreck, as many brides are on their wedding days. This is a fun little party, plain and simple.

The Bride Stands Alone

You also won't be expected to perform the same duties as you would on a traditional wedding day. You won't have to deal with any bridesmaids' tantrums; you won't have a photographer trailing you every second; you won't have to dance with every single guest; and there will be no throwing of the bouquet.

Your duties during your post-elopement reception: Show up, be courteous to the guests, and act a little dignified. Now that's something most newlyweds can definitely handle.

Enjoying Your Post-Wedding Reception

This reception won't be running at a breakneck speed, as many wedding-day receptions do. Many brides find that they are so busy at their receptions—standing in the never-ending receiving line, being pulled in different directions by the photographer and the bridesmaids, being whisked away to dance with seemingly every male in the county—that they barely remember anything that happened. Their memories of the reception are a blur.

This reception will most likely be a more intimate affair. You will actually have the time to eat your meal and enjoy the company of your friends and family—and your husband.

What about Gifts?

You've agreed to your mother's reception idea. You have promised that you will be there and you will be perky, even though it's against every fiber of your being. Now your mother is telling you to register for gifts. Is this a good idea? Can you really do this? Isn't registering something that brides do for their wedding showers and Big Weddings? The answer to all of these questions: It depends on you.

Ⓔ ESSENTIAL

> Although you are the guest of honor, no one is actually obligated to buy you a gift—so if some guests show up empty-handed, you are not allowed to direct them to the nearest department store. You should also make a point to thank the guests who do bring you a little something.

A Word on Etiquette

Most women who elope don't have a bridal shower and they aren't deluged with wedding gifts immediately after taking their vows. Upon your return, many friends and family members won't think twice about the gift-buying question; they'll want to pick something up for you and your husband. There's nothing wrong with registering for wedding gifts after you've eloped, especially if there's a reception planned. Don't feel guilty or funny about it. Most brides register for wedding gifts at some point. You're just working on a different timetable.

Don't Be Stubborn

The fact of the matter is, when friends and relatives receive an invitation for a reception for you and your husband, many of them will decide to bring a gift along. And although it's easy to write a check, some folks don't like to give money—they want to make sure your home is well stocked. Unless the invitation to the reception specifically says, "No gifts, please," you can assume that many guests will be bringing a little something along for you—and if your apartment is completely bare, you may want to consider a gift registry.

Don't Assume the Worst

Many women are uncomfortable with the whole idea of registering for gifts—as though it's a way of saying, "Get me this, this, and this." While it's true that some brides do lose their heads when they are handed a list and a clipboard in a department store, many guests want to give you something useful and look for a registry to ease their shopping decision. Your great-aunt Dolly is just hankering to buy something you need for your new home, and by not registering, you're making things very hard for her.

If your mother—or your mother-in-law—is suggesting that you register for wedding gifts prior to the reception, don't jump to the conclusion that she's suffering from some vicarious wedding syndrome. She has your best interest at heart. You are a newlywed, after all, and you will need various domestic aids in your new home (place mats, dishes, silverware, and the like).

Ⓔ ESSENTIAL

Ironically, registering for gifts will help you avoid the appearance of being greedy. Everyone knows you'll need certain items for your home. Many guests will prefer to purchase a necessity for your home rather than hand you a check; that way, they'll know their money didn't pay for a manicure or a pack of cigarettes.

A Registry for Him

In the event that you've been on your own for years and you really don't need a thing for your home, or if your husband's family wants to make sure he's getting some manly gifts, consider registering in a hardware store. Tools are expensive, and if your family and friends want to fill up the gadget drawer or his tool belt, don't argue.

Evan registered in the hardware department of a home store when he married his wife. He says, "I would recommend it to anyone. You know, when you're doing some job around the house, a lot of times you realize you need a tool you don't have, and you have to go out and buy it. It all adds up—and fast. So if someone wants to buy you tools, let them. My uncle bought me a ratchet set for our wedding. My wife rolled her eyes, but I'll tell you what—it was the greatest gift I got. I've gotten way more use out of that set than my wife has gotten out of the china."

And of course, this is an equal opportunity registry. Many women do their own home repairs, so feel free to fill out that registry with him, or by yourself.

Register for Good Times

You eloped to city hall. You've been living on your own for years, and so has your husband. There isn't a single thing you need—except a vacation, which the two of you are saving your pennies for. That honeymoon may be closer than you think. Many travel agencies will set up a honeymoon registry for you. Your friends and family can contribute any amount to your vacation fund.

If this is something you're interested in, don't go wild planning a two-week vacation at the most expensive and exclusive resort you can find. Depending on the locale you've chosen, the entire expense may not be covered by the generosity of your loved ones. While every little bit brings you closer to stepping on that plane and getting out of Dodge for a while, you're likely going to be paying out of your pocket for at least some of your honeymoon expenses.

There are ways to get the most for everyone's dollar when registering for a honeymoon. Think about traveling in the off-season. Another way to stretch those honeymoon bucks is to stick close to home. If you choose a resort within driving distance, for example, think of the money you won't be spending on airline tickets. You'll be able to treat yourselves to those fancy dinners and not feel ill afterward.

Of course, your travel agent is your best resource when registering for a honeymoon and balancing what you can afford with what you're hoping to receive in the way of monetary support. He or she will be able to guide you toward a realistic vacation that won't break your bank no matter how much—or how little—you end up paying out of your pocket.

Drawing the Line

Although it may be in everyone's best interest to go along with whatever your family plans for your post-wedding reception, you are an adult and you do have your limits. You shouldn't be expected to comply with every request. Yes, you should attend a reception that your mom wants to host for you; and yes, if it makes her happy and you can bear it, you should even repeat your vows for her beforehand. However, you are not required to do any of the following:

- Spend your own money on a second ceremony and/or reception you don't particularly want
- Wear the biggest wedding dress in the world because your mom thinks you look smashing in it
- Attend a ceremony that conflicts with the religious beliefs of you or your fiancé

The last item is a big deal. Many times, mothers are upset when their children marry someone of a different religious faith. If it doesn't matter to you and your husband that you worship in different churches—or that one or both of you don't worship at all—it shouldn't be an issue for anyone else.

ⓔ **ESSENTIAL**

If your mother is withholding her approval of your union until it's been blessed by a religious cleric, and it's something you feel very strongly against, then you are under no obligation to stand before a priest or minister to recite your vows.

Chapter 11

Quieting the Naysayers

What's a newlywed couple to do when seemingly everyone in their lives reject their marriage? If the couple has had a long engagement period, they've had time to discuss potential troublemakers and decide how to deal with them. But when you elope, these issues may pop up out of the blue. So what can you do about the naysayers? Are you going to placate them, ignore them, or cut ties with them altogether? This chapter will help you figure out the best way to approach the problem.

Initial Reactions

Even though you know you made the right choice by eloping, there are some folks who are looking at you suspiciously, as though you've just pulled the wool over everyone's eyes. Unfortunately, there will always be people who love to gossip, and your elopement had just given them fodder for months of speculation.

You Must Be Expecting!

Time was, couples would run off and get married when a little one was on the way. Sure, they'd try to play it off as a honeymoon baby, but when a ten-pound baby would be born six months after the wedding, all suspicions would be confirmed. Apparently this happened often enough to make *elopement* synonymous with *pregnancy*.

That was then. In the twenty-first century, unplanned pregnancies are hardly unheard of, and women in this situation often choose not to make the situation worse by marrying a man who would not make a good husband.

Ⓔ **ESSENTIAL**

> Of course, there's nothing wrong with getting married while you're late in the pregnancy. The point is, anyone who thinks you had to run off and get married because of an unintended pregnancy is living in the past. It's an antiquated notion in this day and age.

What Have You Got on Him?

So you and your new husband are an unlikely couple. Opposites may attract, but they're also targets for confused onlookers. The situation is even trickier if one of you is much wealthier or more powerful. People who don't understand how the two of you could have possibly eloped may assume that your marriage resulted from some sort of blackmail—or a confidential agreement that has nothing to do with true love. If your marriage is currently under the neighborhood microscope, it can be difficult to establish a happy home, to say the very least.

Wild Accusations

Your mother-in-law thinks you got her son drunk and dragged him down the aisle. Your husband's sister is convinced that you gave him an ultimatum, and that you were going to dump him if he didn't marry you. His whole family thinks that he just wanted to get married—because of his age or to avoid being alone—and you jumped at the chance to snag him. Or maybe the pregnancy issue has popped up for real; you're expecting, but rumor has it, you went and got yourself pregnant so he'd marry you.

The bottom line here is that you're the villain. You're so clever and cunning that you somehow hypnotized this man, convinced him to sign a marriage license (which his mother wants to see, just to make sure it's really his signature) and repeat some vows. His family apparently believes that he could not have done this if he had been coherent.

You have your work cut out for you. You're not going to win these people over with any sort of actual evidence—like the fact that he was the one who wanted to elope, or that big diamond ring he presented to you at the altar, or even a videotape of him grinning as he recited his vows, with nary a shackle in sight. Right now, your best bet is to lay low for a while.

Ⓔ ALERT!

Yes, you're angry about his family's behavior, and rightly so. But actively fighting with your husband's family—calling names and hurling accusations—is only going to ensure that there will be ill will between you for a long time.

Handling the Negativity

So what are you to do if your own marriage is up against this kind of scrutiny? Obviously, if the two of you are happy together, it speaks loudly for itself, and that's the most important thing. Having a blissful newlywed atmosphere inside your home is all you really need to be concerned about. Sometimes it's easiest to just ignore those inquisitive eyes peeping at you as you walk down the hall of your apartment building.

A Change of Scenery

Ignoring speculation from coworkers and neighbors is often easier said than done, and if you can remove yourself from the hostile atmosphere, you and your marriage might be better off in the long run.

Maybe you were thinking about moving or changing jobs even before you eloped and became the focus of everyone's attention, but you're bound and determined to stay now just to show everyone that you're tougher than they are. Don't play this game. Think about what's best for you and your sanity and your marriage. Your new neighbor might also be married to someone who *seems* completely wrong for her—to everyone but her, that is.

Ⓔ FACT

If you haven't called his mother any ghastly names, you'll be 100 percent in the clear. She'll be the one making amends to you. Even if she pretends she never acted so horribly, she still won't have anything to throw in your face, expecting you to apologize for the way you reacted to her.

Let Things Slide a Little

If your husband's family has gone off the deep end, think about the position your husband is in, too. He doesn't want this war on his hands for the rest of his life. He loves you; he loves them. But he loves you more, which is exactly why you're going to try to be the better person in this situation.

The fact that his family (or his group of friends) is behaving like a bunch of lunatics is not lost on this man, no matter how nonchalant he's acting. He knows he made the right choice by marrying you; this is your chance to prove yourself not only to him, but to those lunatics as well. When everything settles down, they'll realize that he married you because he intends to spend his life with you—not because you slipped him a mickey.

Shutting Down the Rumor Mill

Take the pregnancy-rumor scenario. If you actually have a due date and are uncomfortable about the whole situation—you keep hearing different rumors, each one a little worse than the previous speculation—one very easy way to eliminate more gossip is to be completely open and honest: "Yes, I'm having a baby. No, it's not the only reason we got married. Yes, we are very excited. No, there's nothing else I'd like to tell you."

Ⓔ ESSENTIAL

Don't reveal any information simply because you feel pressured to. Remember: You are never obligated to disclose anything about your personal life to anyone. It's your business and your prerogative to share it—or not. End of story.

Consider the Sources

Above all, you have to realize that anyone who's attacking you and your marriage is wrong. The only two people who truly know what goes on in a marriage are the two people in it. Outsiders who gossip and take bets on the date of your supposedly impending divorce are saying much more about themselves with their behavior than they could ever say about you.

Friends Behaving Badly

As though adjusting to married life weren't hard enough, you find yourself listening to your close friends and family members telling you what a mistake you've made. Why are they doing this? Have they truly lost their minds? Do they want to see you cry? Would you ever in a million years say these same things to a friend of yours?

Take just a minute and turn the tables. Try to see things from their point of view. You don't need to go so far as to agree with them (in fact, even if you do agree with anything they say, keep that to yourself for now), but it might help ease your mind to understand why they're acting this way. They may snap out of it, or they may continue to act horribly for months. You can only control your perception of the situation and your reaction to it.

No, you're not the worst friend in the world because you eloped in secret. And no, you're not the wickedest woman on the planet because you didn't tell his parents you were getting married. This has much more to do with them than with you.

Ⓔ QUESTION?

Why must your friends behave so badly?
Take into consideration the motives behind any negative comments or bad vibes coming your way. Cut the issue right down to its core: Your friends are human beings. Everyone looks at a situation from his or her point of view, which is tainted by his or her own life experiences.

What's Really Going on Here?

You have a friend who is not only honest about the fact that she thinks your elopement was unwise, she also seems determined to undermine your relationship with your husband. You've confided in her about your rough newlywed adjustment period and instead of giving you a pep talk, she's ready to set you up with someone new. She can't find a single good thing to say about your husband, and she hardly acknowledges the fact that he exists.

The explanation here may be jealousy. Jealousy can take on many forms. It may not be that she wants your husband for her own; it could be that she wants the stable life you've found. Or she may be angry about the fact that you only have time for your mate these days.

She honestly doesn't understand why you can't meet the girls for a drink on Friday night—*sans* hubby.

A real friend will support you and your marriage, even if she doesn't particularly like your husband, because she knows that in reality, your marriage is actually none of her business. Sure, you can cry on her shoulder, and yes, you can look for advice, but a true friend will support your decision; she won't try to convince you that you're wrong for loving this man (unless, of course, there are issues of abuse or he's stolen money from you or he's done something else along those lines). It's that simple.

Any "friend" who is seemingly determined to make you doubt your marriage needs to be cut out of the loop—and fast. The less information she is given, the less damage she can do to your psyche and/or your relationship. Lay low on this friendship until she's ready to accept your marriage as permanent.

Ⓔ FACT

An unsupportive friend may have had one too many bad relationships, so she thinks you're a sucker, or she hasn't had any meaningful love affairs and doesn't understand what the fuss is all about. You may have a hard time explaining the whole concept of "till death do you part" to her.

Lingering Negative Vibes

Once you get past the initial shock of the gossip and rumors surrounding your elopement, you may think you're in the clear. Unfortunately, you may not be. Because you've eloped with a man who is very near and dear to others, those others might give you a hard time for months or years to come. Expect it and prepare yourself for it, and realize that in the end, you can only control your behavior.

Kinfolk Concerns

Every family is different. Depending on the family you've been born into—or the one you've married into—you could be dealing with any one of literally scores of issues. The only one that really matters at this point, of course, is whether your elopement is being accepted as a legally binding relationship between you and your spouse. If it isn't, consider the source(s).

A sister-in-law who is unwilling to speak to you after you've eloped with her brother may be a little bratty—if, for example, she feels threatened by an outsider joining the family. This may be the case especially if things are going smoothly enough with the rest of the clan. Sisters are sometimes fiercely protective of their brothers; they feel as though they have a special place in their brother's lives, and when someone like you drags him off to elope (as she will tell her friends), you hurt their sibling relationship.

It doesn't matter if any of this is actually true. Spencer eloped with his girlfriend, and found the toughest critic to win over in his family was his much younger sister, who claimed to have been "replaced" by Spencer's new wife.

Says Spencer: "My sister is eleven years younger than I am. Honestly, we never had a lot to do with each other, except for living in the same house until I went to college. If she was my little brother, I probably would have had more of a relationship with her, but I wasn't really into playing dolls when I was a teenager and she was a little girl. When I got married, she was a teenage girl, and we had nothing to say to each other at that point.

"So to hear her tell my wife how close we had been until I eloped was hysterical. And you know, the rest of the family knew it wasn't true, but they all thought she was having some kind of episode or something, so no one said anything. The truth is that she behaved that way so everyone would pay attention to her instead of my wife."

Ⓔ ESSENTIAL

This behavior isn't limited to teens, and it's also not limited to girls. Brothers-in-law are also capable of rotten behavior. As in Spencer's family, though, it's often a ploy used by family members to garner attention for themselves. If you're getting along fine with the other family members, avoid the bad seed. Things will work themselves out eventually.

Spencer offers hope for tortured new brides: "It took about three years, but my sister loves my wife now. She thinks I'm married to the coolest chick in town—and I am, by the way—and she calls my wife for advice on everything. She and I still don't have much to talk about, and she kind of pretends that whole 'I hate your wife' thing never happened."

And What about His Friends?

Oh, his friends hate you. They think you somehow lured him into marriage (perhaps with promises of CDs and beer?) and that you only married him to come between them and him, as though you have nothing better to do with the rest of your life.

Can you ever win these clowns over? More importantly, should you try? Up until this point, the discussion has focused on how to handle less-than-eager family members and what to do about your own friends. All of that is actually relatively easy because these are relationships that you have a hand in—whether you want your hand anywhere near those people or not, they're family now. It's in your best interest to come to a peaceful arrangement with them.

Some of your husband's friends won't talk about how romantic your elopement was, but they may call your husband a chump, or other unprintable things. They won't understand that your man wants to come home after work instead of meeting the guys for their weekly billiards tournament; they'll say you have him under your thumb (or, again, they'll use more colorful and highly inappropriate phrases to express their sentiments). They may be hostile toward you, because you have taken their bud from them. And you thought his mom had a hard time letting go. . . .

Here's where you can and should expect your husband to step up to the plate in your defense. If his friends are verbally abusive concerning his relationship with you, your husband needs to put a stop to it, right then and there—preferably the first time it happens.

Ⓔ ALERT!

There's a difference between real nastiness and a little lighthearted ribbing from the guys. If his pals are generally decent fellows who have taken to teasing your husband about his need to call you every ten minutes (which is very sweet, but perhaps a little annoying as far as they're concerned), there's no need to fly off the handle.

The ugly truth is out there: Friends really can be incredibly destructive to a relationship if there's any confusion as to where allegiances lie. They had him first, they'll say, and they know all of his dirty little secrets, which they're only too eager to tell you. They also know exactly how to push your buttons, so try not to let these little boys get under your skin.

One thing you should try to avoid at all costs is reaming out your husband in front of his friends. You'll be putting yourself in a spot. His friends will sympathize with him, try to convince him that he did nothing wrong, and encourage him to misbehave again. When he comes home, feel free to remind your husband that you're his number one priority now—and don't blow your top if it takes him a month to fully accept that.

United You Stand

The best and strongest statement the two of you can make is to stick together. Don't allow your relationship to be undermined by family or friends. You chose to elope because you're crazy about each other. Don't let any negative rumblings damage what the two of you have; it's too precious.

Create Your Own Oasis

No one will argue that dealing with negative feedback on your marriage is awful. You're deliriously happy to be your husband's one and only, and all you're hearing from every other person in your life is, "You'll be sorry." You and your husband will naturally want to talk about this, because it is a big deal—no matter what you tell yourselves.

Set aside one place where you don't discuss the topic of annoying in-laws or intrusive friends. For example, don't let every dinner turn into a gripe-fest. And whatever you do, don't drag your family and friends' comments into your bedroom. The two of you need to have time to work on your new marriage without the constant reminder of the cold world outside your door.

When you set aside a territory that's just for the two of you, you're accomplishing a couple of things. First of all, you're giving yourselves a break from the whole scene—you know that when you settle in to this spot, you won't have to try to explain what your mom really meant when she called your husband "smarmy." Secondly, you're letting each other know that your marriage means enough that it deserves this break. No one else is allowed into this inner sanctum.

Be Happy

You may be surprised at how your mood starts to lighten if you allow yourself to be happy. It sounds silly, but think about letting go of everything that accompanies a negative reaction to your relationship. That means you'll throw away the guilt your parents have piled on you, you'll throw away the doubt your friends have tossed your way, and you'll throw away the anxiety that has been building as a result of all the negativity you've been facing.

Try this for one day: No doubt, no guilt, no fear, and no anxiety. Go back to that moment before you married your husband and relive those emotions. Once you remember why you married him in the first place— because you love him more than anything, because you didn't want to live without him anymore, because you want to spend the rest of your life with him—chances are you'll realize that this is how you should feel and that no one has the right to take that happiness away from you.

Remove Yourselves Temporarily

If you didn't have the opportunity to take a honeymoon, now might be the perfect time. Even if you don't need a week in the sun, you do need time to regroup and redefine yourselves. You know what's waiting for you back home now; this is a time to work on who you are as a couple without the intrusion of family and friends.

Ⓔ ESSENTIAL

If you've had a really brutal time of it with the folks back home, go the extra mile for this trip. Make sure the two of you have time for fun and time to relax.

While you don't want to mire your honeymoon with constant discussions about how to deal with everyone back home, you can't completely ignore the situation, either. It'll still be there when you get back, and sometimes distancing yourself from your family and friends is the best way to figure out how to deal with them.

Packing Up

On a more permanent note, sometimes leaving town for good is your best option. Your parents have been awful to your husband for the better part of a year; his parents refuse to acknowledge your existence. Holidays have been a nightmare, and your weekends are spent separated from each other as he trudges off to see his parents, and you mope off to see yours.

Ask yourself this: Is this helping anyone? The answer, of course, is no. Sure, it's keeping both sets of in-laws relatively quiet, but it's not bringing them any closer to accepting your marriage. You kiss each other goodbye every weekend and holiday just to keep your parents happy—but how does it make the two of you feel? You need to establish your own home and your own traditions at some point.

There's obviously a difference between parents who need some time to accept your marriage and parents who have declared loudly that your spouse is not welcome in their home—not now, not ever. Often such seething hostility results from prejudice; if this is the case, it's going to take an event along the lines of a lightning strike to effect a change of opinion in his parents or in yours.

Ⓔ FACT

It isn't easy to leave your family behind, and no one is suggesting that you won't feel some guilt or doubt. But it may not be possible to have a happy marriage and both families in the same twenty-mile radius. Be honest with yourself and with each other; you both know your families' habits and their chances for change.

As hard as this has been up until now, when you have children, it may be ten times worse (and that's a generously low estimate). Your kids will have one set of grandparents who won't acknowledge the child's mother and another set of grandparents who won't allow the father's name to be spoken in their home.

Sometimes it's for the best to pick up and leave town. Perhaps the opportunity will present itself in the form of a job transfer or a business opportunity out of town; or maybe the two of you will have to actively seek work elsewhere, which is a far more difficult decision to make, especially if you're both content with your jobs. However, if your marriage is on the line, it may be worth looking into.

Ask yourself what you want for your marriage in the long run. Is it better to stay in an area where both of you will always be subjected to this type of hostile environment, or is it better to make a fresh start somewhere else? Only the two of you can answer this question—and when you do, be completely realistic about your expectations for the future.

Chapter 12
Happily Ever After

Couples who elope may miss out on the emotional preparation for marriage. The engagement period is there for more than just worrying which wedding dress to purchase and which guests to invite to the reception. It's also a good time to ponder on what married life is really going to be like. Maybe you've skipped out on this, and now you find yourself in for a crash course in Marriage 101. Don't worry! With a little determination and a little help along the way, you'll pass with flying colors.

Back to Normal Life

Elopements are rife with drama. Leaving town, getting married on the hush-hush, coming home, letting everyone know—you just can't predict how anything will turn out. Every new step is precarious; you're caught up in a whirlwind of romance and intrigue. You've just become accustomed to that knot in your stomach—from anxiety, lovesickness, and fatigue—when you realize that it's gone. Where do you go from here?

We're Married

With all of your covert operations and romantic plans, you may have started to feel like an undercover agent, planning your top-secret elopement and barreling into his mother's living room to mark your territory. Or maybe that's not quite how it went. His mother made tea and you showed her the pictures of your mountaintop ceremony while she cried.

Either way, life with your mate has been interesting, to say the least. But this morning you woke up to realize that *this is it.* It's the *rest of your life* and it's not filled with last-minute flights and weeklong honeymoons. It's just everyday life.

First, you should realize that this happens to most couples—it's the nature of living with someone day in, day out. Even the couples who never thought they'd settle down into quiet domesticity often find themselves living in the midst of polite coexistence with one another; after a certain point, there's no more nightly swinging from the chandeliers.

Secondly, you must realize that it's within your control to keep the romance going. Often, the reason that romance falls by the wayside is because couples get so busy with life that they don't make the time for a walk in the woods together, or they put off a weekend trip together for something that pops up at the last minute—work, family issues, a leaky bathtub, whatever.

Ⓔ ALERT!

Don't fret a little waning romance—that's normal and part of adjusting to a life filled with obligations. But don't let it slide too far off track either, or it may be difficult to recapture that spark when you do find the right time.

You're Not the Only One

Don't fool yourself into thinking you're the only confused newlywed in the world. Because you're expected to be insanely happy at this time, you may feel as though no other bride in the world has ever felt so disoriented. Well, you're wrong. Look at everything that's changed in your life and everything you're dealing with now. You have a husband; you're making a new home together; you're trying to win his family over; he's trying to win your family over; you're both trying to win each other's friends over. On top of all of this, you have a career to consider and you're completely exhausted. If you can take a deep breath and realize that this tumultuous time won't last forever, you're going to feel a lot better a lot sooner.

ⓔ QUESTION?

Do you think you should be able to smile your way through all of this?
Be honest with yourself. You haven't done this before; you're flying by the seat of your pants, and mistakes will be made. Give yourself a break and don't expect perfection.

Talk It Out

Assuming you're not catching a lot of flak from your best friend about your elopement, talk to her about the way you're feeling. Or corral your sister or your mother—again, assuming they're not giving you a hard time about your new marriage. It might really help to talk to someone who's been happily married for several years. She'll be able to tell you that everything you feel is normal, and she might also be able to give you some great advice on keeping the romance alive.

Family Finances

Once the whole whirlwind of being newly married winds down, set aside some time to chat about your finances and everything that goes along with this topic. Although you'd love to, it's going to be hard to get through life pretending you don't need to know where your cash is and where it's going.

You're a team now. These issues are not only fair game for discussion, it's essential that you work together and not against one another. For example, are you planning on building a room over the garage for a work-at-home office, while he's planning on spending that money on a fishing trip? Trouble ahead!

Talking Money

Money is one of those topics many couples like to avoid because it's a volatile issue. If you're a saver and you married a spender (and you didn't realize how big a spender he really is until recently), you know exactly how it feels to discuss your long-term financial goals with a brick wall.

Money can bring you together and it can rip you apart, depending on how closely your saving and/or spending philosophies match up to one another and how well you're able to compromise. If one of you is bleeding the savings account dry while the other is trying to pump new life into it, you need to sit down and discuss the offender's spending habits.

The two of you must come up with a solid plan—a budget—for your household. Start out by listing your income. Then list your bare necessities, things you can't avoid paying for (utilities, car payments, gas, food, rent, and so on). If there's anything left over, you can discuss appropriate expenditures for life's little extras.

Be candid and honest with each other. If you think he's too cheap, say so nicely—and don't be offended when he calls your spending habits into question.

Ⓔ **ESSENTIAL**

Don't beat around the bush on the topic of money. One of you should not walk away from this discussion thinking that it's all right to go out and buy a convertible for use during the summer months while the other walks away thinking that you'll treat yourselves to take-out once a month.

Who Owns What?

If you didn't have a prenuptial agreement drawn up in the doorway of the wedding chapel in Vegas, don't feel too badly about it. Many couples don't take the time to divvy up their assets as they're in the process of eloping.

If you have definite ideas as to where the money you're earning is going to go, lay it out for your husband. If, for example, you're putting all your cash into an account for a down payment on a vacation home, he needs to know that, because not only is he going to wonder why it seems as though you're not being paid, he may go ahead and make another huge purchase, counting on your paycheck to cover the cost.

You're married now; you presumably trust one another. You need to know where your collective money is going, which means you need to talk about your plans for the future. End of story.

Work Issues

Are you willing to do whatever it takes to earn promotion after promotion? Are you, in other words, a workaholic? There's nothing wrong with being a go-getter as long as you've married someone who understands and accepts that. Nothing will put your marriage on edge faster than his sudden realization that you work eighty hours a week and have no intention of slowing down.

Of course, he has his own job, which may involve long hours, weeks on the road, and yearly transfers. Talking about what the future may hold and how it's going to affect both of you is crucial. You may have had no intention of ever leaving your current job—but if you plan on always living in the same city as your husband, you may have to start thinking differently.

Updating and Organizing Your Paperwork

You have a spouse now. Do you need to add him to any of your work benefits? If you're not sure, it won't hurt to meet with someone in your human resources department.

If you're taking your husband's name, you will be undertaking the mundane, time-consuming, and sometimes very frustrating task of calling any business that has ever known you as Ann Smith and alerting them to the fact that you are now Ann Jones. Better to take care of it as soon as possible. Set aside an afternoon devoted to this purpose. If you let it go too long, you may never feel like doing it. Take care of it while it's still a thrill to say, "I'm no longer Miss Smith—I'm Mrs. Jones!" And make sure to contact the Social Security Administration, so that when tax season rolls around, the Internal Revenue Service can match your return to your new name.

If you have life insurance benefits, you'll probably want to make your husband the beneficiary now (tell your mom you're sorry that she's being replaced). And the two of you will need to draw up wills—a grim task, to be sure, but you'll feel better about the whole process after your lawyer explains what happens to a surviving spouse in the event that the deceased spouse didn't have a will.

On the Home Front

While some couples never even consider sitting down and discussing their domestic life, it's a good idea to address the issue early on in your marriage. You wouldn't want to be completely shocked years down the road when your husband announces that you're not returning to your job after you have children. Many couples address these issues before they walk down the aisle, so if you haven't gotten around to it yet, it's time to talk seriously. The sooner you and your husband know where you stand on common household issues, the smoother things will go when those issues rear their little heads.

Division of Domestic Duties

You may have married a man who's sensitive to your needs, but the real question is this: What does he do with his dirty clothes when he comes home from work? If you're tripping over dirty laundry every evening, this is a good time to talk about household chores.

For example, he may be leaving his work shirts where they fall because he expects that you're going to do the laundry. Little does he know that not only will he be doing some of his own laundry, but that technically speaking, doing the laundry doesn't include scooping filthy clothing off the floor.

If you have absolutely no intention of cleaning the house every night when you return home from a long day at the office, say so. The entire household was once the woman's domain, but that was when she was home all day long. Keeping the house ship-shape *was* her job.

Ⓔ FACT

Even if you work from a home office, you can't be expected to dust in between teleconferences. And even if you're home raising children no one should expect the house to be squeaky clean at dinnertime. Kids make messes. That's their job.

If your intention is to hire a cleaning lady, check back with that budget the two of you drew up together. If your finances can support a little household help but your husband strongly objects to this expenditure, perhaps he will be willing to help out with the weekly scrubbing of the floors.

Home Repairs

Many women assume that their husbands can fix things. This is what men do, isn't it? They putter around with their tools on the weekend, hoping something in the house blows a fuse or a gasket.

Surprise! A lot of men can't tell the difference between a fuse and a gasket, let alone replace either one of them. This is a topic that you might want to address before the toilet starts leaking, if for no other reason than to alleviate your dismay at having to call a plumber. Know what your husband is capable of fixing—and what he has no business touching.

On an equal-opportunity note, many women are quite handy with a wrench and a pair of pliers. If you're going to work on installing the new sink while your husband takes care of something else, great—whatever works for you.

Do You Want Kids?

And if you do, when do you want them, and how many are you expecting? Some couples leave this decision up to fate, saying, "If and when it happens, it happens."

If your finances can support a surprise baby, there's nothing wrong with that. If, however, you're scrimping just to pay your grocery bill for the two of you every week, you're going to want to come up with a more solid plan.

Not only are kids an added expense in the way of food and clothing (hard to believe, as little as they are), you're also going to have to plan for child care. Maybe you'll want to stay home, or maybe you need to find a good day care provider. Either option means a restructuring of your finances—there's no way around it.

Ⓔ ESSENTIAL

A lot of mothers are eager to get back to work after they have a baby, and a lot of fathers would rather see their wives stay home with the kids. It's much easier to discuss these issues before you have the baby. Since child care can be a hot-button topic in many marriages, it's never too early to start hammering out this arrangement.

Newlywed Trials

Even if your elopement and your return home have gone more smoothly than you could have ever hoped for (your parents were happy; his parents were happy; no one has you pegged for a blackmailer), adjusting to life together isn't always a cakewalk.

If you are dealing with negative feedback on your new marriage and sparring with your new spouse, it's easy to start questioning your decision to elope. Before you do, realize that every couple has a "breaking in" period—even those who had a two-year engagement.

Maintaining the Romance

Life leading up to elopement can be so romantic. All you want to do is look at each other, all you're thinking about is being together forever, and you just know these feelings will last for the rest of your lives.

What you're not thinking is that reality will have to sneak back into the picture at some point. When you return home and you both have to deal with setting up your home (or finding one), your families' reactions to your marriage, the laundry, the bills, and work, something's got to give. Romance is usually the first thing to take a hit.

It has to happen at some point. It doesn't mean that he's not interested in your every thought, and it certainly doesn't mean that he doesn't love you. It means that you're moving into Real Life together. The romance came so easily when you eloped. Now you have to make romance happen and find new ways to show your love to each other. The good news is that you only need to use your imagination:

- Pick a night during the week when the two of you will turn off the phone and leave your work at the office.

- Give him a coupon book with tickets for massages and foot rubs (and whatever else you think he'd enjoy).
- Try out a new restaurant once a week or on the weekends.
- Don't bring your work to bed with you—let your bedroom be a sanctuary for the two of you.

Your lives are busy. Make sure neither of you are letting your relationship slip just because it's so easy to allow it to happen.

He Has Weird Habits

What's more disconcerting to a newlywed woman than learning that her husband has to count everything? Or discovering that he talks to himself—he has actual two-sided conversations—as he shaves in the morning? How about those "lucky socks" he likes to wear on Wednesdays?

 **ESSENTIAL**

This is where your sense of humor comes into play. Unless he's exhibiting signs of living in his own little world (those voices in the bathroom have different accents, for example), try to see his unique habits as endearing—the very things that make him the person he is.

Actually, there are far worse things for a bride to deal with. A little compulsive behavior can come as a shock for a woman who had no idea that she'd be searching for his requisite toothpicks after every meal. He seemed so normal before you moved in with him.

Sure, your husband has a few quirks, but doesn't everyone? If he's kind and loving and the man of your dreams—aside from those socks—try to let these things slide. And then he won't comment on your rather obsessive need to have egg salad for lunch every day except Monday—which is, of course, chicken salad day.

His Habits Are Just Gross

Nothing can kill the romance of a new marriage faster than seeing his toenails on the bathroom floor, or finding stubble from his razor right next to your toothbrush on the bathroom counter or all over the sink. The toilet seat is up, there's laundry all over the place, and he leaves dirty dishes on the floor. Who is this man? He seemed so hygienic before you married him.

Realize, first of all, that he is not the first man to lose his manners after successfully wooing a woman to the altar, and he won't be the last. Realize, too, that this is strictly a personality thing; there are women out there who gross out their husbands with their little habits, too.

Must you resign yourself to a lifetime of wearing tennis shoes in the bathroom to protect your delicate feet from the shards of toenails littered across the floor? Or will you have to be his cleaning lady from now on, just so you can live in your own home without the fear of moldy food lurking under the sofa?

First, take an honest assessment of your own personality. If you have been called a neat freak your entire life, chances are you might be overreacting to at least some of his behaviors. If, on the other hand, you have never been one to scrub anything with bleach, you don't clean the house just for fun, and yet his habits disgust you, chances are you have a valid concern.

Talk to him. Explain that you are not going to pick up after his every move, and that you *do* expect him to clean up after himself. Write up a checklist for him, if it helps. List the pertinent items: Please clip your nails over the garbage can, please put your laundry in the hamper, please eat your food in the kitchen, and so on.

Ⓔ **ALERT!**

You may not want to hurt his feelings, but if his rather icky habits are affecting the romance in your marriage, he needs to know it. That's a big issue, and not something to gloss over in the name of sparing him any emotional discomfort.

What Have I Gotten Myself Into?

Quirky behavior is one thing. A complete change in behavior, on the other hand, can mean trouble in a relationship. Meeting his friends for the first time and being forced to accept the fact that your husband actually likes these creatures can be a real kick in the head, too. But before you overreact, calm down and step outside the situation for a minute. Get your bearings. It's probably not as bad as you think.

He's Just Different Now

Does your new husband bear very little resemblance to the man he was—or the person you suspect he was only pretending to be—while you were dating? Many couples are on their very best behavior during their courtship. He never raised his voice to anyone before you were married; now he seems to be angry at the world and not afraid to let everyone know it. You, meanwhile, fell in love with his Mr. Sunshine persona—where does that leave you now?

Ⓔ ESSENTIAL

Don't write him off as an imposter just yet. He may need time to get used to his new status as a husband. He has undeniable responsibilities now, and he realizes it.

If you dated for a very brief time, you may be in for a surprise. This might be who he really is; but if you were together for any significant period of time, it's more than likely that you really do know who he is, and that he might be going through a rough period right now.

Marriage is a bigger step for some people than for others—and even though he really loves you, the realization that he's in a committed, now-and-forever relationship might be the thing that's on his mind. Or perhaps his concerns are financial: How are the two of you going to buy that big house you've got your eyes on? How is he going to advance in his career when he only wants to be with you? Lest this all sounds sexist, many women are prone to the same worries after marriage; saying, "I do" is a big deal regardless of gender.

We Can't Get Along!

So everything is coming to a head in your new home—the messes, his bad mood, your devastation at thinking that maybe you made a mistake in marrying this guy. Hold on. Don't go looking for trouble. Step out of your situation for just a minute and realize that you're both in the middle of a huge life change.

You're going to need an adjustment period—time to get used to the idea of having a spouse to whom you are each accountable, time to settle in to your new home, and time to work out your schedules so that your contact isn't limited to a goodbye peck on the cheek in the morning. This may all sound incidental. If you love each other, all of these things will work themselves out, right?

Yes, they will—whether they work themselves out in a positive manner or a negative one largely depends on the effort the two of you put into your relationship. Chances are, you already know someone whose marriage or long-term relationship didn't work out. Many times the reason is that the one or both parties involved just didn't make time for their relationship.

Simple Solutions

So what are you to do if your new husband is getting on your last nerve and/or he seems like a stranger since you pledged your life to him? Communication is your first and best action. Get everything out in the open. Take turns talking; don't interrupt. If you need to, schedule a block of time for this conversation. Turn off the phone, don't answer the door, and don't walk out of the room until you're both finished. Nipping things in the bud is always better than allowing annoyances to stew.

 ALERT!

Having an open mind means that neither of you will be on the defensive. Remember, you're trying to eliminate problems, not create new ones. Lay some ground rules for constructive criticism and airing of various concerns, and you'll walk away from your talk feeling better about where your new marriage is headed.

Opening the lines of communication is a useless venture unless both of you come to the meeting with open minds, willing to listen to the other person's grievances. Don't attack each other; speak in a calm voice, and really think about what the other person is saying. Is it possible that you do talk on the phone way too much, especially when he's waiting to cuddle up with you at the end of a long day? Hear what he's saying here: His complaint isn't about the long-distance bill as much as it is about his wanting some time with you before he falls asleep.

When It's Time for Counseling

Depending on whom you ask, counseling is either a last-ditch effort to ward off divorce or a pre-emptive strike on marital problems. Couples who are engaged to be married are sometimes encouraged to attend premarital classes, which address everything from finances to intimate relations. If you didn't have the benefit of a premarital class, and your engagement was nonexistent, you may feel completely overwhelmed. Couples counseling might be a good alternative.

If you've grown up in a household where *psychoanalysis* was a dirty word, you may just write off counseling as something for truly troubled couples; the partners involved can't get along because they're both mentally ill. Not true.

Counseling is for anyone—of any economic status, any age, any race, and at any point in marriage—who has questions or concerns about their relationship that are not easily resolved. It is not for the mentally ill.

Where to Find Help

Obviously, if your family is adverse to the whole idea of counseling, you don't want to ask their advice on the issue of finding a therapist—and they wouldn't know where to steer you, anyway. Picking a name from the phone book (or the Internet) is risky. Counseling is about finding a qualified professional to meet your needs; the right fit is crucial.

If you don't know anyone who's been to a counselor and/or you want to keep this a personal matter, ask your primary-care physician for some guidance. Not only will she know in which general direction to send you, her office may also be very helpful in finding a therapist that accepts your insurance, or locating a counselor who has weekend or evening hours.

Hold Your Head Up

There is no shame in asking for help if you feel you need it. In fact, you should pat yourself on the back for seeking out assistance when it would have been much easier to let things slide. Looking for a counselor when you need one says a lot about your feelings for your husband and your marriage; you're in this for the long haul. You want it to be a happy long haul.

Appendix A
Additional Resources

Here is a quick list of Web site links and books to help you as you plan your elopement.

Helpful Web Sites

✍ *www.usmarriagelaws.com*
   Incredibly complete guide to the laws and procedures governing marriages in the United States, Canada, the Caribbean, and Europe. Includes information on waiting periods and requirements for obtaining a marriage license.

✍ *www.co.clark.nv.us/clerk/marriage_information.htm*
   Thinking of hopping a plane to Vegas? You can apply for your marriage license online at this Web site. It also contains pertinent information on planning your elopement in Clark County.

✍ *www.chapelsoflasvegas.com* and
✍ *www.vivalasvegasweddings.com*
   One industry, one city, many, many Web sites to choose from. These two offer a good overview of what's available for your Las Vegas wedding, including unusual and/or classy settings and wedding packages.

✍ *www.lvchamber.com/visit/tipping.htm*
   Includes advice on Las Vegas tipping.

✍ *www.sandals.com*
   A look at one popular couples' resort offering an all-inclusive island wedding package.

www.weddingstheislandway.com

Loads of information for couples interested in saying, "I do" in the U.S. Virgin Islands.

www.expedia.com

Looking to book your elopement trip right this very minute? Log on and see which flight is leaving town next!

www.thediamondbuyingguide.com

A useful resource when you're looking to buy the rings. Includes a diamond-buying quiz, helpful definitions, frequently asked questions, and information on shopping for jewelry online.

www.guide2jewelry.com

Exposes little-known insider information on the jewelry industry, so that you will be better prepared to make an informed purchase.

www.smartmoney.com

Offers a worksheet on the Home Buying Primer page of the Real Estate section (listed under "Personal Finance" on the home page) that allows you to plug in your own numbers (income versus debt, in a nutshell) and find out what kind of home you can really afford.

www.homestore.com

Offers a similar home-buying calculator on the Home Finance page.

Further Reading

How to "I Do": Planning the Ultimate Wedding in Six Weekends or Less, by Holly Lefevre and Christine Cudanes. Regan Books, 2000.

Wedding Readings: Centuries of Writing and Rituals on Love and Marriage, by Eleanor C. Munro. Penguin USA Publishing, 1996.

One Hundred and One Classic Love Poems. McGraw-Hill/Contemporary Books, 1998.

Love Poems (Everyman's Library Pocket Poets), by Sheila Kohler and Peter Washington. Knopf, 1993.

Saving Your Marriage Before It Starts: Seven Questions to Ask Before (and After) You Marry, by Leslie Parrott. Zondervan Publishers, 1995.

What No One Tells the Bride: Surviving the Wedding, Sex after the Honeymoon, Second Thoughts, Wedding Cake Freezer Burn, Becoming Your Mother, Screaming about Money, Screaming about In-Laws, Maintaining Your Identity, and Being Blissfully Happy Despite It All, by Marg Stark. Hyperion Press, June 1998.

Appendix B
Tipping Guide

You're on your wedding trip or honeymoon, and it seems as though everyone has a hand out. Are they checking for rain or waiting for a buck or two? The following is a general tipping guide that may help you figure it out.

Tipping Guide	
Bartender	$1 per drink
Wine steward	15–20 percent of the wine bill
Waiter	15–20 percent of the bill, depending on the service
Buffet servers	$1–2 per person if the service was good
Room service	15–20 percent of the bill (if not already included)
Chambermaid	A couple of dollars a day (left at the end of your stay)
Bellboy	$1–2 per bag; $1–2 for opening your room; $5 for errands
Concierge	$5–10
Doorman	$1–2 for hailing a cab; $2–5 for helping with bags
Valet	$2–3
Skycaps	$1–2 per bag; $5 for exceptional service
Casino dealer	Placing a bet for him or her once in a while
Keno and bingo runners	$1–2 every now and then, even if you aren't winning

Index

We Have EVERYTHING!

BUSINESS

Everything® **Business Planning Book**
Everything® **Coaching and Mentoring Book**
Everything® **Fundraising Book**
Everything® **Home-Based Business Book**
Everything® **Leadership Book**
Everything® **Managing People Book**
Everything® **Network Marketing Book**
Everything® **Online Business Book**
Everything® **Project Management Book**
Everything® **Selling Book**
Everything® **Start Your Own Business Book**
Everything® **Time Management Book**

COMPUTERS

Everything® **Build Your Own Home Page Book**
Everything® **Computer Book**
Everything® **Internet Book**
Everything® **Microsoft® Word 2000 Book**

COOKBOOKS

Everything® **Barbecue Cookbook**
Everything® **Bartender's Book, $9.95**
Everything® **Chinese Cookbook**
Everything® **Chocolate Cookbook**
Everything® **Cookbook**
Everything® **Dessert Cookbook**
Everything® **Diabetes Cookbook**
Everything® **Low-Carb Cookbook**
Everything® **Low-Fat High-Flavor Cookbook**
Everything® **Mediterranean Cookbook**
Everything® **Mexican Cookbook**
Everything® **One-Pot Cookbook**
Everything® **Pasta Book**
Everything® **Quick Meals Cookbook**
Everything® **Slow Cooker Cookbook**
Everything® **Soup Cookbook**
Everything® **Thai Cookbook**
Everything® **Vegetarian Cookbook**
Everything® **Wine Book**

HEALTH

Everything® **Anti-Aging Book**
Everything® **Diabetes Book**
Everything® **Dieting Book**
Everything® **Herbal Remedies Book**
Everything® **Hypnosis Book**
Everything® **Menopause Book**
Everything® **Nutrition Book**
Everything® **Reflexology Book**
Everything® **Stress Management Book**
Everything® **Vitamins, Minerals, and Nutritional Supplements Book**

HISTORY

Everything® **American History Book**
Everything® **Civil War Book**
Everything® **Irish History & Heritage Book**
Everything® **Mafia Book**
Everything® **World War II Book**

HOBBIES & GAMES

Everything® **Bridge Book**
Everything® **Candlemaking Book**
Everything® **Casino Gambling Book**
Everything® **Chess Basics Book**
Everything® **Collectibles Book**
Everything® **Crossword and Puzzle Book**
Everything® **Digital Photography Book**
Everything® **Family Tree Book**
Everything® **Games Book**
Everything® **Knitting Book**
Everything® **Magic Book**
Everything® **Motorcycle Book**
Everything® **Online Genealogy Book**
Everything® **Photography Book**
Everything® **Pool & Billiards Book**
Everything® **Quilting Book**
Everything® **Scrapbooking Book**
Everything® **Soapmaking Book**

HOME IMPROVEMENT

Everything® **Feng Shui Book**
Everything® **Gardening Book**
Everything® **Home Decorating Book**
Everything® **Landscaping Book**
Everything® **Lawn Care Book**
Everything® **Organize Your Home Book**

KIDS' STORY BOOKS

Everything® **Bedtime Story Book**
Everything® **Bible Stories Book**
Everything® **Fairy Tales Book**
Everything® **Mother Goose Book**

LANGUAGE

Everything® **Learning French Book**

Everything® **Learning German Book**

Everything® **Learning Italian Book**

Everything® **Learning Latin Book**

Everything® **Learning Spanish Book**

Everything® **Sign Language Book**

MUSIC

Everything® **Drums Book (with CD), $19.95 ($31.95 CAN)**

Everything® **Guitar Book**

Everything® **Playing Piano and Keyboards Book**

Everything® **Rock & Blues Guitar Book (with CD), $19.95 ($31.95 CAN)**

Everything® **Songwriting Book**

NEW AGE

Everything® **Astrology Book**

Everything® **Divining the Future Book**

Everything® **Dreams Book**

Everything® **Ghost Book**

Everything® **Meditation Book**

Everything® **Numerology Book**

Everything® **Palmistry Book**

Everything® **Psychic Book**

Everything® **Spells & Charms Book**

Everything® **Tarot Book**

Everything® **Wicca and Witchcraft Book**

PARENTING

Everything® **Baby Names Book**

Everything® **Baby Shower Book**

Everything® **Baby's First Food Book**

Everything® **Baby's First Year Book**

Everything® **Breastfeeding Book**

Everything® **Father-to-Be Book**

Everything® **Get Ready for Baby Book**

Everything® **Home-schooling Book**

Everything® **Parent's Guide to Positive Discipline**

Everything® **Potty Training Book, $9.95 ($15.95 CAN)**

Everything® **Pregnancy Book, 2nd Ed.**

Everything® **Pregnancy Fitness Book**

Everything® **Pregnancy Organizer, $15.00 ($22.95 CAN)**

Everything® **Toddler Book**

Everything® **Tween Book**

PERSONAL FINANCE

Everything® **Budgeting Book**

Everything® **Get Out of Debt Book**

Everything® **Get Rich Book**

Everything® **Homebuying Book, 2nd Ed.**

Everything® **Homeselling Book**

Everything® **Investing Book**

Everything® **Money Book**

Everything® **Mutual Funds Book**

Everything® **Online Investing Book**

Everything® **Personal Finance Book**

Everything® **Personal Finance in Your 20s & 30s Book**

Everything® **Wills & Estate Planning Book**

PETS

Everything® **Cat Book**

Everything® **Dog Book**

Everything® **Dog Training and Tricks Book**

Everything® **Horse Book**

Everything® **Puppy Book**

Everything® **Tropical Fish Book**

REFERENCE

Everything® **Astronomy Book**

Everything® **Car Care Book**

Everything® **Christmas Book, $15.00 ($21.95 CAN)**

Everything® **Classical Mythology Book**

Everything® **Einstein Book**

Everything® **Etiquette Book**

Everything® **Great Thinkers Book**

Everything® **Philosophy Book**

Everything® **Shakespeare Book**

Everything® **Tall Tales, Legends, & Other Outrageous Lies Book**

Everything® **Toasts Book**

Everything® **Trivia Book**

Everything® **Weather Book**

RELIGION

Everything® **Angels Book**

Everything® **Buddhism Book**

Everything® **Catholicism Book**

Everything® **Jewish History & Heritage Book**

Everything® **Judaism Book**

Everything® **Prayer Book**

Everything® **Saints Book**

Everything® **Understanding Islam Book**

Everything® **World's Religions Book**

Everything® **Zen Book**

SCHOOL & CAREERS

Everything® **After College Book**

Everything® **College Survival Book**

Everything® **Cover Letter Book**

Everything® **Get-a-Job Book**

Everything® **Hot Careers Book**

Everything® **Job Interview Book**

Everything® **Online Job Search Book**

Everything® **Resume Book, 2nd Ed.**

Everything® **Study Book**